MORTAL FOLLIES

MORTAL FOLLIES

Episcopalians and the Crisis of Mainline Christianity

WILLIAM MURCHISON

Encounter Books New York • London

First American edition published in 2009 by Encounter Books,
an activity of Encounter for Culture and Education, Inc.,
a nonprofit, tax exempt corporation.
Encounter Books website address: www.encounterbooks.com

Manufactured in the United States and printed on
acid-free paper. The paper used in this publication meets
the minimum requirements of ANSI/NISO Z39.48Ð1992
(R 1997) (*Permanence of Paper*).

FIRST AMERICAN EDITION

LIBRARY OF CONGRESS CATALOGING-IN-PUBLICATION DATA
Murchison, William P.
Mortal follies : Episcopalians and the crisis of mainline Christianity/
by William Murchison.
p. cm.
Includes bibliographical references and index.
ISBN-13: 978-1-59403-230-1 (hardcover : alk. paper)
ISBN-10: 1-59403-230-0 (hardcover : alk. paper) 1. Church renewal. 2. Epis-
copal Church–Forecasting. 3. Christianity–21st century. I. Title.
BV600.3.M87 2009
283'.73090511–dc22

2008048048

For Nancy

Contents

O Almighty God, who hast built thy Church upon the foundation of the apostles
and prophets, Jesus Christ himself being the chief cornerstone:
Grant us so to be joined together in unity of spirit by their doctrine,
that we may be made an holy temple acceptable unto thee; through
the same Jesus Christ our Lord, who liveth and reigneth with
thee and the Holy Spirit, one God for ever and ever.

—*The Book of Common Prayer,* Collect for the Sunday closest to June 29

Prelude

YOU MIGHT SAY WE HUMANS HARDLY EVER NOTICE PEAKS—— financial, political, cultural, physical, and so on—until we find ourselves descending from them: down, down, into strange valleys, step by step, sometimes head over heels. Once, it was bright, blazing noon; suddenly, clouds and darkness gather.

A particularly brilliant example of such a peak is America's golden summer of 1929, on the eve of the stock market crash—a summer when, as the discerning (if, alas, largely forgotten) novelist John P. Marquand related, "the only clouds on the horizon were the roseate prophecies of an even more roseate future." Then, like a thunderclap—

We will understand this peak and valley business, if we take the trouble to think about it, as the universal human experience, sometimes stated as, "You win some, you lose some." One difficulty, for many, lies in watching that experience play itself out in relation to the church of God, whose walls are widely assumed to shelter the eternal, the lasting, and the true—the things of heaven—from ordinary human give-and-take and interference.

1

Can the church, like any ordinary institution, both soar and fall? We know that it can. We have watched its descents and plunges, its slumbers and snoozes, for as long as there has been a church—something like two thousand years now.

Early in the twenty-first century after Christ, in the United States of America, as in Western Europe, we are watching another of those ecclesiastical plunges: down, down, from confidence, mission, and a gratifying sense of general acceptance, into disorder of the most disheartening sort. Whereas the United States remains, broadly speaking, a religious nation—one of the world's *most* religious nations—more and more of the religious decide for themselves what to believe, what store to set by those beliefs, such as they are, and what the terms of human life ought to be. A 2007 survey by the Pew Forum on Religious and Public Life, released in 2008, declares that most religiously committed Americans take "a non-dogmatic approach to faith," persuaded as they are that their own religion isn't the only way to salvation. A gently pluralistic view of things: calm and democratic, if not precisely, in conventional terms, *religious.*

On abortion, as surveys have shown for years, a majority of Americans reject, in whole or in part, Christian teachings on the sacred character of an unborn life: in which rejection various Christians, not a few of them ministers, join with gusto. Marriage and marriage relationships, once deemed subject to divine regulation, have fallen under secular domination—so much so that many public officials have undertaken to define marriage in new ways, discovering no reason it should not apply to couples of the same sex. Often, in the century's first decade, to take in the news was to get the notion that the defining isssue for American Christians was the suitability, or the disgrace, of marriage rights for homosexuals.

The idea that public schools could or should allude to God in describing the work of creation is in many modern eyes scandalous and un-American. For that matter, paganism, heresy, and outright atheism have been winning respectful hearings, not least on bestseller lists. The new century was but a few years old before authors such as Richard Dawkins and Christopher Hitchens began reaping lucrative rewards on account of excoriating God, declaring him either imaginary or irrelevant. Surely a sign of anxiety, if not of something more serious, concerning our old sacred commitments was the furor several years ago over the novel and movie *The Da Vinci Code*, a sort of feminist fantasy about a conspiracy to suppress the discovery of—*shh!*—the "truth" about that celebrity couple, Jesus and Mary Magdalene.

Another reminder of the withdrawing religious tide is the semi-civil war that seems to break out every December. The issue: whether a modern American should bite his tongue before wishing another American a merry Christmas. No one fifty years earlier could possibly have foreseen such an odd and jarring circumstance.

A new vogue commences meanwhile. Christians identified by the media as "progressive" have taken to emphasizing environmental and "justice" issues over moral issues once understood as central to Christian witness: abortion, for instance.

Who is to blame, assuming "blame" is the right word? Various Christians couldn't be better pleased by what they see as Christianity's spirit-led growth into new ways of understanding God and His revelation. They might recognize the church's present journey as a descent from the peak of that ecclesiastical prosperity which marked the 1950s. Just as likely, they would say, *fine* (if not *cool*)—high time an old church joined the modern world.

And speaking of "about time," I need to declare my present purpose, my rationale for tugging at the reader's sleeve. It is, broadly speaking, to talk about the ravages that modern times have wrought upon Christianity in the United States. More narrowly, it is to speak of how often, how extensively, and with what dismal results, the churches themselves have egged on the ravagers.

No one, I grant, fully reforms a church from outside it, though kings and potentates have tried. For a church to change at its deeper levels, the consent and encouragement of the church itself must be had. If modern American churches are divided against themselves, if human occasions and human hopes no longer depend as they once did on the church's blessing and guidance, if popular entertainment increasingly criticizes or derides churches and the people inside them, if society thumbs its nose at churches and hints we'd be as well off without them, then the churches can hardly exempt themselves from responsibility.

A prime cause of ecclesiastical malaise in the twenty-first century is the appreciation, sometimes the outright admiration, that Christian churches show for the mores and modes of the secular culture: the arts, academia, politics, journalism, the entertainment industry. Especially is this true at the priestly and ministerial level, where political and economic sympathies closely correspond to those usually found in the universities, the arts, and the media. Ministers are, in cultural terms, verbalists, wielders of words, talkers, and writers. They relate well to other verbalists, less well to sweat-of-the-brow types like the merchants and engineers and homemakers who, on Sundays, gaze back at them from the pews.

Between pulpit and pew a gap of sorts perpetually exists, a function of the fundamentally different outlooks of the ministering and the ministered-to. Lately the gap seems more cultural than anything else, a matter of politics and what modern people call their "lifestyles." At the start of the present cultural struggle, the impulse among many American Christians was strenuously to resist. As time passed, resistance waned. Thoughtful souls began to wonder whether the culture might be right about the things it once seemed monumentally wrong about.

Was it possible (was it not certain!) that the Lord was doing a new thing, without the applause He deserved from his own representatives on earth? As more and more Christians conformed their outlooks to those of the secular culture, the president of the Southern Baptist Convention—a fellowship comparatively untroubled by cultural trends—acknowledged that "culture has transformed us into its own image."

The declining participation in Christian worship during the past forty years isn't due wholly to Starbucks and Sunday morning talk shows. It stems as well, depending on what church we're talking about, from growing irritation over projects and obsessions better suited to political than theological remediation. A first-rate example would be climate change; another, abolition of capital punishment.

Hand in hand with the tendency to mingle cultural and religious mores comes comparative indifference to certain landmarks of Christian belief and action—the uniqueness of the Christian revelation; an explicit call (from Christ, actually) to make disciples of all; the duty to name and rebuke sin; monogamous heterosexual relationships as the Christian standard; divine authority (e.g., Holy Scripture) as dispositive in worldly matters. Such notions as these could seem unwise or unworthy to Christians afraid of pressing "exclusivist" claims on a pluralistic society. Why, no, that wouldn't be attractive at all in an age of radical individualism and moral "choice," coupled, curiously, with a form of moral absolutism about certain ideals, the whole hatched in the insurrections of circa 1965–1973 against war, capitalism, parents, moral restraints, college deans, and the social order of the day. The Methodists over time bought in; likewise the Presbyterians; many Catholics as well; some Baptists. And did *we* ever buy in—we Episcopalians.

Ah. I hadn't previously mentioned it. Well, then: Episcopalian I have been for nearly all my adult life. (My youth was Methodist, as was my wife's.) Episcopalian my family and I remain for at least—a nice semi-poetic word here—the nonce. My enterprise, between these covers, concerns "mainline" American churches broadly, the Episcopal Church more narrowly—the Episcopal Church as a lens for viewing and coming possibly to understand better the present diminished state of American Christianity. I do not mean diminished in sublime importance under the aspect of eternity. I mean diminished in terms of unity and effectiveness in ministry and witness. A church struggling to understand its nature and purpose is a church radically impaired in the eternal contest over human allegiances.

Not all of American Christianity is impaired. Even non-Christians know that. Churches of all sorts thrive in all sorts of places. Roman Catholicism, which benefits from the presence of America's large Latin American immigrant population, continues to grow, as does the Pentecostal persuasion. Mormons, generally regarded as outside regular Christianity due to certain of their beliefs and interpretations, outnumber Episcopalians and Presbyterians put together. Many an individual "Bible" church, unaffiliated, often as not, with a particular denomination, and specializing in recreational as well as spiritual outreach, hums with energy. Of a Sunday morning, cars overflow their parking lots and spill onto the neighborhood streets.

If only the same could be said of the so-called mainline denominations: United Methodists, Presbyterians, Episcopalians, Lutherans, and Congregationalists! It is strange to observe the present tribulations of these bodies, which so recently constituted America's "Protestant establishment," awash in members and money. No longer.

Consider the United Methodists, down to 7.9 million members in 2008, compared with more than 11 million in the late 1960s. Consider the Evangelical Lutheran Church in America, off 1.58 percent from the previous year, and the Presbyterian Church (U.S.), down 2.36 percent. Think of my Episcopalians: off 4.15 percent for the year; reduced in overall numbers by more than a third from their mid-sixties peak. Ponder the United Church of Christ, the Congregationalists, down 1.2 percent to barely a million members; less than a fifth of the booming Mormon population. The same Pew Forum survey that showed such airy indifference to doctrinal p's and q's asserted that barely three fifths of mainline Christians find religion "very important," with a mere 26 percent committed to weekly church attendance. Nearly a quarter of mainliners told the pollsters they go to church "a few times a year"—just often enough, apparently, to keep the driving directions fixed in memory. Writing in *First Things*, Joseph Bottum has gone so far as to declare the old "Protestant America"—that nation forged by the combined witness of the major Protestant denominations—to be dead beyond the power of resuscitation.

For the tribulations of the mainline denominations, no single explanation, no single set of explanations, can fit every case, not in this large and various republic, and in this eclectic time, so accommodative of so many varied outlooks and aspirations. Some of the perplexity, for instance, is demographic—a sociological matter, one might say. One indisputable reason for the shrunken number of Episcopalians is that Episcopalians have a very low birth rate. We take in this point appreciatively. Then a question intrudes: *Why* do Episcopalians have a very low birth

rate? Has it to do with the present beliefs and attitudes of Episcopalians, shaped by their own current theology?

I put it forth as truism that eventually everything gets back to
beliefs. Beliefs form and shape actions. Actions (as whose mother
has not reminded him?) have consequences. It is mainly of beliefs
that we must talk in trying to sort out the woes of contemporary
mainline Christianity. What beliefs, then—the doctrinal ones? Of
course. Partly. Yet beliefs come in all sizes and varieties, having
to do with dinner plans and political preferences as well as with
the relationship between faith and works and the efficacy of
infant baptism. We will talk about belief, generically. But in what
context?

The context of one particular church, the Episcopal Church.
I will in some sense talk of all the mainline churches by talking
of one. That is my project. We need first to understand, insofar
as space permits, the *context* in which American Christianity
functions. That context is the culture of the twenty-first century,
not only its religious and spiritual side, but also—perhaps just as
often—its secular side, whether understood as disdainful of religion or merely detached from questions of origin and destiny.

I think we best understand the "mainliners" as cultural
chameleons, melting so completely into the secular culture as
sometimes to vanish from view, except when enduring in-house
embroilments over the speed or extent of the vanishing process.
On the one hand, chameleon-like behavior is nothing new in
Christian annals: less the exception, perhaps, than the rule. On
the other hand, the present culture—so louche, so free form, so
resistant to notions of truth and constancy—sets out ghastly traps
for the bumbling.

That is one side of the matter. There is another, more imposing
side. A culture of emptiness invites—*dares*—others to fill it. To
precisely this task the Christians of the Roman world addressed

themselves, with vast and enduring success. It can't happen again? Who says so, apart from the Christian chameleons for whom the cultural norms of the twenty-first century seem warm and comforting enough, worth sucking on as bitter winds howl?

It's oh, so true. One chameleon, after a while, will begin to look like the rest. How much in that event do we gain by inquiry into the almost complete disappearance of the Episcopal Church into the cultural woodwork? More than one might casually suppose, I'm prepared to argue.

Part of the delight, if one can call it that, of examining the Episcopalians proceeds from their prodigious prominence in American history, their inherent attractiveness to many minds outside the fold, and, last, to their newly realized gift for imaging, and blowing up to poster size, the aggravations of the religious moment. We are like Walt Whitman—large, containing multitudes.

ONE

Sunset and Evening Star

A ND YET, BEFORE WE CAN START TO SEE WHERE WE ARE, WE
have to look with some attention at the places where we
have been.

Nor need we travel far to get there. Many of us carry around
intimate memories of the decade known as "the Fifties." Others
know the period by its legends, whether of repression, cultural
twitching, or *hi-honey-I'm-home* complacency. A point easy to
miss about the 1950s is that the period was deeply complex, neither one thing nor the other (as indeed might be said, in varying
degrees, of all human eras).

I was there. So were many who read these words, and may
appraise differently the factors I lay out for consideration. On one
point we might agree. It is that whereas the 1950s fairly tingled
with religious energy, and worshippers overflowed the churches,
and to some observers the Kingdom of God seemed ready to
break forth right here in the good old U.S.A., there was much
more to be taken in—restlessness, disquiet, a growing sense of
agitation.

The years that followed the defeat of the Axis Powers, and of the Great Depression as a notable bonus, were as good, seemingly, for American churches as for America itself. Everyone (so you might have guessed from externals) wanted to be a Christian. Returning veterans sought to get on with normal life, as they remembered or envisioned it. The church was a large part of that quest, holding out possibilities of community and fulfillment—and sometimes even of that spiritual redemption that churches were in business to encourage.

As families expanded with the onset of the baby boom, steeples rose and pews multiplied to accommodate their needs. Religion, one might have said, was in fashion, possibly to a degree previously unknown even in a country proud of its longtime sacred commitments. By 1960, a truly flabbergasting 69 percent of Americans claimed membership in a church. Certain automatic assumptions filled the lungs. Of the new lawyer or teacher or store manager in town, someone was sure to ask, in a welcoming spirit, "Where do you go to church?" Not, "*Do* you go?" The only conceivable question was, "Where?" It was a genial form of recruiting, and it expressed the social conviction that the place to be on Sunday mornings was in God's house.

Popular culture, being popular, was suffused with religion—anyway, a sort of religion, obscuring more often than highlighting doctrinal differences. Where the customers led, the entertainment industry followed. The early Christian martyrs figured centrally in successful movies like *Quo Vadis* and *The Robe*. Charlton Heston parted, then un-parted, the Red Sea, to the admiration of millions who lined up to see *The Ten Commandments*, never mind their personal views on the original document.

Television, then coming into its own, offered as spiritual commentator and guide the eloquent Roman Catholic Bishop Fulton

J. Sheen, whose weekly program, "Life is Worth Living," began its influential run in February 1952. The program drew immense audiences, quickly landing Sheen on the cover of *Time*. Another consequential personality was the popularizing Protestant minister Norman Vincent Peale, whose book, *The Power of Positive Thinking*, published the year of Sheen's television debut, purported to establish a vital link between religion and success, a link never long out of sight in American business culture. There was also—powerfully, unforgettably—the Rev. Billy Graham, inviting the world, in fervent gospel preaching, to find and affirm its Savior.

New possibilities arose. Was it not time for Christian soldiers of every denominational variety, to march onward in unity? The National Council of Churches was the great cooperative venture that twenty-nine denominations, representing 33 million Christians, launched in 1950. The Episcopal bishop who was its first president spoke of the NCC's goal: "a Christian America in a Christian world." (Could any other statement by a public figure so starkly demonstrate the distance between the sixth decade of the twentieth century and the first decade of the twenty-first?)

Congress played its own part in the religious revival, making us, via the Pledge of Allegiance, "one nation under God." President Dwight D. Eisenhower himself declared that "our government makes no sense unless it is founded in a deeply felt religious faith—and I don't care what it is." The remark, despite exciting ridicule on the part of some theologians, was aimed, not inaccurately, at a broad and sensible consensus.

And yet were matters as good as they looked? If at the popular level, religion—Christianity in particular, seemed the going thing, many "professionals"—theologians, pastors, priests—felt an unease bordering on discomfort. Were the churches doing what churches ought to be doing? Was it enough that people were showing up in increasing numbers for a closer walk with God? Perhaps, just perhaps, more was indicated.

As various professionals saw it, a great deal more was indeed indicated. A bubble needed puncturing—the bubble of popular complacency and social comfort. The war had not long been over when an Episcopal priest, the Rev. Theodore Wedel, had intimations that all this might be so. In a series of lectures published in 1950, just as the National Council of Churches was beckoning forward the massed ranks of Christian soldiers, Wedel lamented that "Christianity is today, among a majority of educated men and women, including many nominal Protestant Christians, an almost unknown religion."

Unknown? How would that be, amid the bustle of masons and carpenters aggressively throwing together new churches? To Wedel's mind, "Golden Rule idealism," "moralism," and biblical ignorance had become features of the religious landscape hardly less common than new white-painted steeples. "Main Street Christianity" was "a kind of Christianity without theology, one which does not repudiate the name of God, but which has basically little to do with him."

Many shared Wedel's apprehensions. The Jewish theologian Will Herberg found America's "common religion" to be nothing less than the American way of life, "the operative faith of the American people." With a "spiritual structure," yes—one that "embraces such seemingly incongruous elements as sanitary plumbing and freedom of opportunity, Coca-Cola and an intense faith in education—all felt as moral questions relating to the proper way of life." God functioned, said Herberg, "as sanction and underpinning for the supreme values of the faith embodied in the American Way of Life." It all amounted, he thought, to "secularized Puritanism, a Puritanism without transcendence, without sense of sin or judgment."

The bestselling sociological commentator Vance Packard declared wincingly that most Americans saw church attendance as "the nice thing that people do on Sundays. It advertises their respectability, gives them a warm feeling that they are behaving in a way their God-fearing ancestors would approve, and adds (they hope) a few cubits to their social stature by throwing them with a social group with which they wish to be identified." A desired "social group"! Did anyone mention the Episcopal Church, with its ancient silver plate and gilt-edged membership rolls? There was some of that going about; there would be much more.

The Christian churches were rising—slowly, gradually, but emphatically—to critique, if not to flagellate, the culture from which they were receiving such hearty back thumps of fellowship and encouragement. There might seem some oddness in this, except for the greater oddness we will note as we go along— that of the churches' coming to embrace cultural norms more hostile to traditional Christianity than anything on display in the postwar 1950s.

From the straight course the churches were making toward Scylla they tacked suddenly, pennants flying and canvas fully stretched, toward Charybdis. The 1960s began with thoughtful churchmen asking how the church might more fittingly identify itself with the culture's genuine needs. The decade ended in religious warfare of a new kind. It seemed the churches of Jesus Christ were more than disappointed with the old culture; they were angry at it, and at its continuing manifestations—angry and ready to see in the old culture's place a new cultural style altogether. As course corrections go, that of the American churches, in the 1960s, was something to behold, not least for velocity and noise.

Just what was it the churches felt, increasingly, called on to do? This took some working out. Methodists, Presbyterians, and the like, closely tied to the hard-working middle classes, took their time when it came to stirring. An Episcopal tradition of social commitment, observed irregularly but generally with heart and spirit, did begin to assert itself in the 1950s.

In a generalized sense, one Episcopal theologian, Norman Pittenger, had in 1950 called for "an awareness of the privilege of Christian discipleship . . . a consciousness of the fact that one *is* a Christian, called to a peculiar kind of life and a unique loyalty to the divine imperative." Yes, but what then? The sociologist Peter Berger, in *The Noise of Solemn Assemblies*, published in 1961, identified the "what" as "Christian outreach to the distressed." Indeed, said he, it was more than that. The call, a loud one, was to "modify the social structure itself," and to erect "Christian signs in the world." Not billboards—rather, plain evidences of Christ's presence in the world. There had to be "complete identification," Berger argued, with the conditions of daily life.

So also argued the Rev. Gibson Winter, Episcopal priest and professor at the University of Chicago Theological School, whose influential and much-quoted book, *The Suburban Captivity of the Church,* published the same year as Berger's, called for repudiation of the model of the church as refuge and resting place. *No!* cried Winter. The church was a place for *exertion.* The manifest duty of America's churches, he said, was to create "a human environment in the metropolis." "The churches," he affirmed, "must now become publicly accountable institutions with a vision of the metropolis and their mission to it." Service to purely middle-class interests could no longer suffice, if ever it had. By such a model the church was "an island of conformity in the metropolis—a treadmill where men and women grind out their salvation." Such an "introverted church" was a contradiction in terms. The church had to turn outward, in love and reconciliation. The church of Jesus Christ had, in short, to take itself, and its purposes, with utmost seriousness.

This was no extravagant claim. Most Americans understood, vaguely at least, the extent to which the Christian churches had influenced the course of their history, from the theological empires of New England where the anti-slavery crusade germinated, then on through the push for Prohibition. Particular ministers and laymen had attached themselves fervently to the cause of laboring Americans—preaching, urging a Social Gospel, a message of justice.

First had come the Congregationalist minister Washington Gladden (1836–1918), with his ringing appeals on behalf of the rights of labor. There followed the outspoken, and even more influential, American Baptist minister Walter Rauschenbusch (1861–1918), who read the Scriptures as a condemnation of "socialized, institutionalized, and militant" evil that "the Kingdom of God and its higher laws" could displace "only by conflict." To which end he foresaw "prophet minds" fighting "for the freedom of the people in political government and for the substitution of cooperation for predatory methods in industry."

In the years following World War II, the call to engage the world often fell upon willing ears, of which one set belonged to a young Episcopal priest with extraordinary credentials—a wealthy family, a Yale degree, and a Silver Star and Navy Cross awarded for gallantry on Guadalcanal. The Rev. Paul Moore, as he would write later, was "drawn to the cause of the poor and the persecuted." With solemn intentions, this scion of a prominent New York banking family sought ministry, his young family alongside him, in slums, and downtrodden places. The world needed the church—that was Moore's idea, and the idea of other Episcopalians like him, including a young Harvard-educated lawyer, William Stringfellow, who moved to East Harlem in order to provide the poor with legal services otherwise unavailable to them.

There was, at least in Anglican—hence Episcopal—thought, strong theological grounding for commitments of this kind. It lay in the "incarnational" understanding of Jesus as the enduring, undying savior, positioned at the center of human affairs, suffering for the sake of all, not merely for the well-born and comfortable who lived in climate-controlled homes, sent their children to good schools, and on Sunday mornings turned up, freshly scrubbed and accoutered, at the nearest Episcopal church. The nineteenth-century English theologian Frederick D. Maurice had embodied this understanding, with concern (as the twentieth-century American Protestant theologian Reinhold Niebuhr epitomized it) for "[t]he conversion of mankind from self-centeredness to Christ-centeredness." Maurice stood against mere "religion"—heartless formalism scarcely cognizant of Christ's kingship. By the 1940s, another English theologian, Alec Vidler, saw theology coming around to Maurice's "emphasis on the solidarity of the human race, on the doctrine of the mystical body of Christ, on Christ's Lordship over all men and his relationship to the whole created order."

Incarnational theology was earthy, material—*incarnational*. That was what was meant by "incarnation": Word made flesh; God here among us, as one of us. The here-ness, the now-ness of Jesus drew reinforcement and splendor from his "real presence" in the Eucharist, the elements of bread and wine rendered flesh and blood in the spiritual sense, the crucified Son of God taken on the tongue of the faithful worshipper. Not that all Episcopalians, or Anglicans, by any means shared this somewhat rarefied understanding. (The low-church style of worship put far greater emphasis on Scripture and sermon than on regular celebration of the Holy Communion, as the Eucharist was then styled in the Book of Common Prayer.) Yet the wonder and power of Christ here among us under the aspects of bread and wine made a powerful appeal to worshippers with hearts turned in the indicated direction. Paul Moore called the Eucharist "the pattern and the power"—"an exchange of our bodies for his body, of the Cross for Resurrection, of captivity for freedom, of death for life, of all else for joy." On this intuition he built a consequential ministry.

As did, to somewhat different ends and purposes, the kinetic, not to say frenzied, bishop who until his death in 1969 would symbolize Episcopal wrestlings and fidgets. James Albert Pike founded no school of thought within Anglicanism, nor did he leave much trace of his compulsive activities, apart from a number of short, glib books that still turn up regularly in secondhand sales. Episcopalians scarcely knew whether to acknowledge him as prophet or provocateur. He was likely, in indeterminable portions, a mixture of both. As charismatic dean, in the early 1950s, of New York City's Cathedral of St. John the Divine, and subsequently as bishop of California, Pike won for himself a large and attentive audience, outside as well as inside Episcopalianism. (For a few seasons he was host of his own local television show.) The man with the large black-framed spectacles and unstoppable mouth, wearing proudly the garments of church office, was given to judgments and observations not generally associated with men of the cloth. It was a major part of his reckless charm.

Surveying the Christian faith at large, Pike, like growing numbers of non-Episcopal kidney, glimpsed mold, encrustation, and piles of rubbish. Old ideas in a new time simply weren't the ticket, not in the eyes of James A. Pike. At the 1964 General Convention, he attacked "outdated, incomprehensible, and nonessential doctrinal statements, traditions, and codes"—a considerable statement from a bishop, sworn like his brothers to drive from the church "all strange and erroneous doctrine."

"The fact is," said Pike, "we are in the midst of a theological revolution. Many of us feel that it is urgent that we rethink and restate the unchanging gospel in terms which are relevant to our day and to the people we would have hear it; not hesitating to abandon or reinterpret concepts, words, images, and myths developed in past centuries when men were operating under different world views and different philosophical structures."

Oh.

Pike, whose visage *Time* magazine featured on its cover (as it had featured that of Bishop Sheen) spoke with some acuity, and certainly fluency, to an age more full of skeptical questions and blunt assertions than of reverent assents. It was an age of hard facts, with yet a high regard for the experts who came in so many guises: television commentators, soapbox haranguers on college campuses, secular politicians, founders of causes. He was all the more in tune with the times on account of his willingness to drink constantly from different springs and wells and chalices just to sample the taste. That he loved the church seems clear enough—though his manner of showing affection outraged a large portion of the church's membership and leadership, who judged him to be putting souls in danger while bringing the church itself into disrepute. In the early 1960s, the Episcopal Church charged him formally with heresy, in response to an accusation by fellow bishops. There was general cringing at the idea of actual attempts to reprimand wrong teaching. Was there not about this whole enterprise the odor of wood smoke and burning martyrs? The church shrank back. Pike walked from his auto-da-fé bearing only a judgment against his theological "irresponsibility."

Which had been considerable.

The bishop of California, it seemed, would say nearly anything that came to mind. St. Paul, to Pike, was "crotchety." Ancient doctrinal formulas such as "came down from heaven" were to the bishop "incredible . . . in this Space Age." The Virgin Birth of Christ he found troublesome "for many intelligent people." The doctrine of the Trinity, one God in three Persons, was "unintelligible and misleading to men of our day." More "unintelligible" by far seems the notion that no harm could come of taking particular Christian doctrines and giving them a swift kick, conveying to listeners the idea that modern folk who held to these ancient Christian ideas really weren't (wink, wink) People Like Us.

Large numbers of American Christians listened. Large numbers nodded, or nodded and chuckled and smiled, with appreciation. On some of the points that streamed forth (endlessly, it began to seem) from Jim Pike and other theological jostlers of elbows, there was room for reservation, if not furious objection. Yes. Of course. But you never could tell. What if, after all, there was something to this new business about straitjacketed thinking and scandalously unpaid debts to the Lord of Life? Consider. If the life of the world could run in new, exciting courses after so much darkness and division, might not understandings of life and eternity be ripe for reappraisal? Might it not be time to . . .

So much for the 1950s, its questionings, quibbles, and persistent sense of unease. The noise of solemn assemblies began to fade. The church—not in every place, by any means, and with many a finger crossed, or set of arms folded in opposition—began to move its stiffened legs. Dead ahead lay the 1960s. Those years would prove decisive.

I am at the Phoenix airport, changing planes as I head home from a West Coast university for Christmas break. The year is

1963. And what is this? A man, possibly a year or two younger than I, hurries past. I turn around. I look. No, the truth is, I *stare*—at a head of hair, thick and loose, the bangs, like window drapes, falling to the eyebrows. It might be a sheepdog, or Moe from "The Three Stooges." Then, as the saying goes, recognition dawns. This is a Beatle. An imitation Beatle, to be sure, but with the same hair we've seen in the newspaper photos relayed from England. One had known there was such hair; one just hadn't expected it outside its proper context, at the Phoenix airport. Suddenly the age of the male flat top and of Bryl Creem ("A Little Dab'll Do You," the TV commercial promised) seemed less certain than before, to the extent one had thought to question its staying power.

It was possibly my first glimpse of that which later we would call "the Sixties." I do not recall the moment as unsettling or premonitory. On the other hand, I find, looking back, no coincidence in the timing. President John Fitzgerald Kennedy had been assassinated barely two weeks earlier, less than sixty miles north of my hometown. The two things I desired most to see on landing that day in Dallas were my father, who was due to collect me, and, on the drive home, the Texas School Book Depository, a helpless monument to horror, surrounded still by gawkers, with index fingers pointed toward the seventh floor. I forgot for a long time about my Phoenix airport encounter. Afterwards, concerning that hinge moment, a great many things came to me, things that were fading even then, though we had no inkling of it, and other things that were putting out small shoots and tendrils.

The times, as a not-yet-world-famous Bob Dylan was to sing (and as we were to hear incessantly afterwards) were a-changing. Equally, as some of the ancient Romans had said, we were changing with those times (*et nos mutamur in illis*).

Was there something new in all this? No change, no *growth*, is the law of life. Yet the changes we were to experience—or *endure*, as the case might be—in the 1960s and afterwards were deeper, darker, and more disruptive than anyone could have foreseen in that deep, darkening fall of 1963.

Older assumptions about life, about norms, about reality itself commenced a slow fade-out. Into focus came new assumptions, rattling alike the windows and the nerves. It was more than just a case of getting used to daily sensations like "campus protest" and "flower power," to cite two popular terms of the time. There was a sense, prevalent among the younger set but shared increasingly by older onlookers that personal expectations suddenly counted much more than seemingly stale viewpoints and definitions. What did parents know, anyway? They were so . . . old! As were their notions about life and how best to get along in it. It was appropriate, seemingly, to live by the slogan, "Never trust anyone over thirty." (Until—naturally—becoming thirty yourself.)

Whatever justice and love and duty and hope had meant previously, these commodities no longer enjoyed special "relevance" (another then-popular term). A certain kind of sensitivity would lead us to the understandings necessary to carry on with modern life. What kind of sensitivity? Clearly the kind that people of sensitive outlook (people such as *us!*) were only too happy to employ. The logic of the new creed was never other than circular: What we say is so because we're the ones saying it! Nor was it likely to be confused with the older wisdom founded on tradition and the slow, careful exploration of possibility and limits. It now seemed the very notion of limits was some archaic fantasy, some artifact in a dark attic made bright by the sudden flinging back of wool curtains.

An older culture was making way, with many a groan and grunt, for a new culture, one whose varied influences radically inform the living of life.

It is common nowadays to talk loosely of "the culture," and of the various wars that rage within it. Learned books are written on the subject. Still, the term gives pause. Many of us think of the word "culture" as pertaining chiefly to artistic pursuits. People who went to the symphony and read books, perhaps even watched subtitled foreign films at the local arts theater, were "cultured." Culture, in that specialized sense, was acknowledged a good thing, at least by those who thought about the matter. Culture stood over against barbarism, or, as some said, Elvis.

As we use the word today, "culture" mainly refers to an environment—moral, political, economic, or whatever, and a set of attitudes, actions, and assumptions associated with that environment. That is the definition I propose for present purposes. I mean by "culture" the ocean and all schools of fish that swim in it. I mean the modes of the larger society, in which institutions of every sort exist: viewpoints, mental habits, and crotchets; entertainments and obsessions, ideas and ideals, norms and nonnorms, behaviors, memories, ways.

To taxonomize all things cultural is clearly not the task of an essayist (my self-definition), but of entire teams of sociologists, aided and abetted by those whom journalists always like to identify in news stories as "experts." My own definitions of "the culture" are bound, for some, to fall short, a certainty I acknowledge with, I hope, appropriate regret. I would say in my own defense that anyone's definition of a beast like "the culture" is bound to fall short. That is how things are. I invite argument and dispute as to terms, even as I implore the reader's patience.

I have advanced the notion that America's "mainline" churches in general, and the Episcopal Church in particular, whether meaning to or not, have placed themselves in at least partial thrall to the culture. I do not mean the whole of one church or another. I do not mean the whole of the culture. What I mean is that prominent, not to say dominant, elements of church and culture now carry on this intimate and destructive relationship.

I need, before going further, to say a word about culture generally and its effects on those fish swimming daily in its depths. The mistake I want earnestly to avoid is that of implying that over here is something called "culture" and over there something called "church," and that the latter lives under some sublime obligation to keep the former always at arm's length. That would be nonsense. Life has never worked that way, for all the occasional efforts of good Christian folk to isolate themselves from grossness and corruption: the desert anchorites, for instance, or the Amish, or even those who merely cultivate stricter standards of personal behavior (e.g., avoidance of "bad language") than the larger society tolerates.

In practice, the church is forever rubbing elbows with, bumping up against, "the culture," striving to infuse it with appreciation of duties and possibilities whose source is other than human will and intellect. Often the endeavor works, the church having the better of such disputes as may follow. In the early twenty-first century, human intellect and, especially, human will seem often to enjoy the upper hand.

Why? I contend we need, for the sake of social and moral stability, to seek an answer too long deferred. We need to seek it likewise for the sake of possibly imperiled souls. The place to start is, I think, with some account of the culture to which Christianity addresses itself, the culture all around us, the ocean in which we swim—or flounder.

If asked to assign our times a hallmark, I would answer by fusing two characteristics.

Characteristic 1. Personal autonomy.

Characteristic 2. Moral fragmentation, if not actual disintegration.

What we want to do we jolly well ought to be able to do, with no one to deny us. That seems, broadly speaking, and with room for numerous exceptions and variations, the nub of the matter. As the journalist David Brooks has limned the attitude: "[T]he core mission of life is to throw off the shackles of social convention and to embark on a journey of self-discovery. Behavior is not wrong if it feels good and doesn't hurt anybody else. Sex is not wrong so long as it is done by mutual consent." This is a picture of life lived without moral structure or all-encompassing purpose, life as we see it all around us.

We are by now deeply "into"—one more post-1960s expression—autonomy and leave-me-aloneness. Autonomy is independence of others and of claims imposed from the outside: by religion, by family, by social code, by almost any institution seeming to communicate preferences of one kind or another. Fine that someone else should prefer a thing. To require of others that same preference—no, no. Not any more. The commercial freedom of the marketplace and the political freedom of the polling place have subtly shaped and formed us.

So have historical events and occasions. The Protestant Reformation, which chopped up western Christianity into discrete fragments, including Anglicanism, gave religious proclaimers of all sorts—some wise and devout, others addle-brained and noxious—title to say whatever they liked to whomever they liked. The scientific achievements of the seventeenth-century could be read as further celebrating individual vision as over against the all-seeing-ness, all-providingness of God. A century later, the thinkers of the French Enlightenment began to heckle and jeer the claims both of church and of state. To the jeering and heckling the French Revolution, which began in 1789, added guillotining. The old regime was not much of a regime: lazy, self-satisfied, open to imputations of corruption and tyranny. It may have deserved strong rebuke. What followed was out of all proportion to offenses rightly or wrongly imputed. For the authority of crown and church the revolution substituted the authority of the mob: loud, bloodthirsty, easy for orators and agitators to manipulate. Appropriating Notre Dame Cathedral to its own purposes, the mob elevated to preeminence the newly created goddess of Reason. It was not precisely what France's own Martyrs of Lyons, in Roman times, had willingly surrendered their lives to affirm—the triumph of human passion over the solemn prescriptions of God.

That which Edmund Burke had called "the red fool fury of the Seine" receded during and after the Napoleonic wars, though not to its former banks. In Britain and America, Victorianism reclaimed some lost ground for Authority. All the same, Victorianism probably encouraged more liberation of one kind and another than it shooed away. That was thanks partly to the romantic movement in art and literature but more particularly to capitalism—the economic handmaiden of democracy—and a scientism (especially Darwinism) that came over time to disdain many of religion's putatively ignorant claims. The unseen God of the Christians took up less and less of modern folks' time and interest. A new form of "critical" biblical scholarship asked questions about the authority of those Scriptures that Christians had seen as reflecting the mind, if not recording the actual words, of the Lord God Almighty.

Still, at the start of the last century, and for some time afterwards, Authority was vertical and top-down in a way that can amaze us when we look back, provided we remember to look back. Tradition, meaning the distilled experience of the past, held considerable sway; so, in greater or lesser degree, did notions of self-denial. Common forms of address ("Yes, sir," "No, ma'am") and gestures of deference ("Ladies first") told their own story. It was a story of cultural gradients. Everyone had the right to an opinion, but some opinions were more sensible than others—were, in fact, not mere opinions but, rather, well-settled statements about the world and its operations; also about the obligations that daily life entailed. It seemed—yes, really—there were duties that particular people owed to other people. One performed those duties because—well, because it was the right thing to do: "right" being a reality, just like the obverse reality of "wrong."

I interrupt these remarks to flush from his Florentine tomb the philosopher-statesman Machiavelli, so that he may give fair warning about nostalgic delusions. "Men ever praise the past," wrote Niccolo, in his *Discourses*, "and find fault with the present." We have to be perpetually cautious, in other words, about unflattering comparisons of present times to past times. All I suggest here is, I think, empirically verifiable. Verticality and top-downness in culture gave way slowly but inexorably to horizontality—a side-by-sideness of ideas, outlooks, postures, assumptions, and beliefs, especially moral and social beliefs. (Disputes over distribution of power and property naturally went on, as irresolvable in the twenty-first century as in the first.) That an idea was old or venerable created no presumption in its favor. To the contrary, age darkened the filaments of the brightest ideas. The new culture read by different lights entirely.

Well before the turn of the present century, democracy, meaning voter sovereignty, passed over from the realm of political theory into daily life. Whatever you wanted, maybe that was after all your *right,* your *entitlement.* Not to the point of anarchy, perhaps, but farther in that tipsy direction than society had ventured before. Counsels of caution, and of respect for the wisdom of the past, got barely a nod from activists laboring at their separate, often uncoordinated, projects. What if, after all, there was no abstract right and wrong? What if there were multiple ways of understanding and embracing truth? What if truth itself was just a conceit invented to keep down the town rowdies? Or perhaps over time we came to see things in a clearer light than our ancestors had done. Bless their hearts, they may have had good cause to believe thus-and-so was right and authoritative, but times changed, information accumulated, new insights formed. The past had no hammerlock on our brains. Thus the periodic duty to sweep from our cultural closets those notions and practices unsuited to a new age. Out came the brooms, and up from different sides of the cultural spectrum went the respective yells of delight and horror.

If the 1950s were far more dynamic and less "conformist" than legend maintains, still it was the decade of the 1960s—hippies, Woodstock, Eastern religions, incinerated draft cards, "Make Love Not War," marijuana and LSD, Black Panthers, the Age of Aquarius—that smashed up older concepts of authority and left them writhing in the street. No longer, it seemed, were particular ideas, particular modes, inherently "better" than others, and therefore more deserving of respect. Shelby Steele has rightly called the 1960s "a time when seemingly every long-simmering conflict, every long-standing moral contradiction in American history, presented itself to be made right even as an ill-conceived war raged on. And the resulting loss of moral authority was the great vacuum that literally called the counterculture consciousness into being."

Not that, prior to the 1960s, Americans had showed much disposition toward forelock-tugging and the automatic ratification of a stranger's "should" or "ought." In this most democratic of nations, champions of the authoritative long ago made a sort of peace with the Great *Oh, Yeah?*—with the right to heckle, deeply ingrained in the American character. All the same, the 1960s were something new in our national experience: a time of defiance, provocation, and exhibitionism for their own sake, of fist-shaking and nose-thumbing all across the cultural spectrum. A favorite exhortation from the late 1960s and early 1970s became, loosely, a kind of watchword for the period: "If it feels good, do it!" To claim that these six words were the creed of a whole culture would be, as with any slogan, going infinitely too far. Still, this particular slogan encapsulated the increasingly common notion that personal choice trumped outdated rules and regulations. The whole appeal to openness and untapped possibility found lodgment in unlikely places, such as the universities and the churches, teaching institutions where the "vertical" approach to knowledge and instruction had generally held sway.

Virtually across the board, choice exerted itself as the determinative factor in art, in music, in self-expression; in courting and marriage and personal relationships; in the use of time itself. In 1973, the U.S. Supreme Court proclaimed the right of an American woman to decide entirely for herself, and without obstruction, the vexed question of whether to bring a pregnancy to full term. In 2003, the justices found it indefensible that Texas should statutorily penalize consensual sodomy, given that (in the words of Justice Anthony Kennedy) an emerging awareness of liberty gave substantial protection "to adult persons in deciding how to conduct their private lives in matters pertaining to sex." The justices sang sweetly of "an autonomy of self that includes freedom of thought, belief, expression, and certain intimate conduct."

In business, said Peter Drucker, "knowledge workers" were similarly in control of their own destinies, could they but see it. Free speech came to embrace, with societal and judicial permission, attitudes like the burning of American flags and the sprinkling of movie and television scripts with words once rendered in the funny papers, delicately if suggestively, as "&!#@$#@."

In time—partly because they seemed to have little choice, partly because the fever of the times carried them away, the teachers loosened up. Perhaps, they started to reflect—just perhaps—the old ways really had grown offensively, uselessly old. Perhaps, as "the kids" were trying to instruct us, it was time for reassessment, reevaluation, growth.

In the meantime, could someone shut the window, please? With all that racket from the street: How could anyone *think*? The noise, of course, was that of metaphorical bricks being hurled metaphorically from below, smashing metaphorical window-panes, scattering metaphorical books, papers, and chalk.

TWO

Love in the Ruins

THE TIME COMES AT LAST TO TURN UP THE LIGHTS ON THE Episcopal Church's present tumult and torture. I grant freely those are not words the national leadership of the Episcopal Church would employ—"tumult" and "torture." The church's national leaders, whether from conviction or professional need just to go on smiling, can be downright chirpy as a venerable ecclesiastical body burns to the ground.

In a 2007 *New York Times* advertisement keyed to the five-hundred-year anniversary of Anglican worship in the New World, church headquarters acknowledged, while strenuously playing down, the news about searing divisions within the fold. "Occasionally," said the ad, with sublime understatement, "[Episcopal] struggles make the news. People find they can no longer walk with us on their journey, and may be called to a different spiritual home . . . Despite the headlines, the Episcopal Church keeps moving forward in mission. . . . We're committed to a transformed world, as Jesus taught: a world of justice, peace, wholeness, and holy living. . . . Come and visit . . . come and explore . . . *come and grow.*"

Come and *grow*? This was curious. Virtually the last enterprise with which anyone would identify the twenty-first-century
Episcopal Church is growth—the expansion of membership rolls
through evangelism, conversion, and like inducements. What tales
were "the headlines" telling about the Episcopal persuasion? One
frequent and persistent tale was of Episcopal worshippers, not
to mention whole Episcopal parishes—dioceses, even—detaching
themselves from the Episcopal Church and its imputed corrup-
tions, repudiating the Episcopal Church's authority and control
over them. It was common by 2008 for these secessionists to seek
the supervision of an Anglican archbishop from Africa, Asia, or
South America—someone believed more deeply wedded to biblical truth and Christian morality than were the bishops of the
Episcopal Church. In the summer of the same year, more than
a thousand high-ranking, theologically conservative Anglicans,
coming chiefly from countries of the so-called "Global South," and
terminally provoked by the spiritual transgressions of American,
Canadian, and English Anglicans, flung down the gauntlet. Hard.
The Global Anglican Future Conference (GAFCON) professed for
the sake of the Christian gospel to be walling off practitioners of
the new theology from the contamination of false and competing
gospels. It was possible, with only a glimmer of imagination, to
see a day coming when "liberal" and "conservative" Anglicans
would find themselves occupying separate, inviolable homes. Or
maybe not. With Anglicans, one can't always tell.

However that might be, Episcopal hierarchs professed
low-level alarm at their church's deteriorating prospects in the
Anglican world. Church spokesmen spread wide their hands.
Why, if hard-nosed conservatives were displeased by what the
church was doing—softening ancient objections to homosexuality, according secular projects priority over theological ones—
well, it was too bad, but maybe the recusant brethren would some

day open their eyes and see what wonderful new things the Holy Spirit was revealing. If they didn't in the meantime go somewhere else or just plain shut up.

Not that developments of this sort sprang from virgin soil. For twenty or thirty years, national Episcopal leadership had behaved as though the culture were its guide, its inspiration, its source of wisdom and truth. Whenever traditional Christianity clashed with late-twentieth-century culture, the Episcopal Church normally weighed in on the side of the culture: for enhanced choice in life, for more laxity and less permanence in belief. The consecration, in 2003, of a partnered gay priest, the poignantly named Vicky Gene Robinson, as bishop of New Hampshire was the definitive signal that for the present-day church there would be no reversal of commitments, no further attempts (save in *New York Times* ads) to portray theological rifts as mere differences of understanding and viewpoint.

Consequences ensued, and made news of a sort generally unwelcome at Episcopal headquarters in the home city of the *New York Times*. If some outward Episcopal splendors remained, along with signs here and there of genuine health and devotion, more noticeable were the indications of malaise and decay. In 1965, the Episcopal Church had boasted more than 3.5 million members. As the twenty-first century began, the United States had a population half again as large as in the mid-1960s, yet a third fewer Americans claimed to be Episcopalians. True, other Christian denominations—so vital, so attractive throughout the 1950s and on into the 1960s—were likewise losing members. Still, the plight of the Episcopal Church was splashed with special poignancy, not to say tragedy.

The church itself reported, on the basis of a 2005 survey, that only 12 percent of Episcopal churches held services that were 80 percent full or better. Thirty-seven percent reported "very serious [internal] conflict" in the preceding five years. The percentage of financially healthy congregations fell during the same period from 56 to 32. Barely half of Episcopal rectors and vicars described themselves as well-versed in the Bible. "Very few Episcopal churches," the report said, "report that their members are heavily involved in recruiting new members."

It was not exactly an environment geared for growth of the sort trumpeted in the *New York Times* ad, or for growth of any other sort! Around the time the survey was being conducted, I chanced upon some statistics concerning a once-potent Episcopal diocese—the one headquartered in Newark, New Jersey, and for years led by a media savvy bishop, John Spong, whose favorite theme was the need for radical overhaul of the Christian faith. It seemed the Episcopal Diocese of Newark, since 1972, had lost 46 percent of its members. Sixteen percent of its churches had closed down forever. Nor, the report went on, had a single new church or mission opened anywhere in the diocese during the past sixteen years. The picture was of ecclesiastical rigor mortis, of flies buzzing about a waxen countenance.

Six months later, at its General Convention in Columbus, Ohio, the church chose as presiding bishop a woman, the Rt. Rev. Katharine Jefferts Schori, whose initial sermon to the convention hailed "our mother Jesus" (a "metaphorical" reference, she tried later to explain) and called for the church to focus on poverty, health, and "sustainable development." Further, lay and clerical deputies declined an invitation to affirm their belief in Jesus Christ as the only way to salvation. It was as if the U.S. Chamber of Commerce had refused a chance to affirm the blessings of capitalism, and its debt to Adam Smith. Or, no—it was more. The deputies were quarreling, by implication, with the One identified in their church's creed as "Maker of heaven and earth . . ."

Many Christians, I think, might want to ask, what goes on with the Episcopal Church? What, in heaven's name, actually *does* go on?

Quite a lot goes on. But first, a related question demands attention: Does whatever goes on in just one church, regardless of history and methods, truly matter?

I hope to make clear in due course that it matters considerably. This is partly because the Episcopal Church, on account of its outsized prominence in American religious affairs, and its membership in the worldwide Anglican Communion, matters considerably. Episcopal affairs matter, furthermore, because the trap into which the Episcopal Church has stepped, with eyes wide open, as it happens, is one into which the other mainline denominations have inserted a foot at least part way. The trap of which I speak is commitment to the ways and means of twenty-first-century culture as surrogate modes of following Jesus Christ. The Episcopal story is a cautionary tale, and cautionary tales have applicability beyond the circumstances from which they spring.

This is just such a tale—for Christians of varied persuasions, including those who may wish, some pages on, to hurl at me the nearest potted plant or wine glass. A distinguished historian—and Episcopalian-since-turned-Catholic—noted over a decade ago the common thread joining the varied stories of today's mainline denominations. The churches, wrote Thomas Reeves, are becoming "uncertain guides in a civilization starving for lack of purpose and solid moral and ethical guidelines." "Solid teaching," Reeves wrote, "is at a premium, and the basics about sin, repentance, judgment, and hell frequently go unexplored. . . . It is all too often presumed that God is wholly and merely . . . nice." Just the right kind of God for us, one might say—a God likely to win the approval of a culture that carefully avoids offending subcultures viewed as emerging from repression.

A culture of "liberation"—the one we now live in—presents itself as perpetually at war with the remnants of the unliberated culture dominant until the mid-1960s, after which, miraculously, everything became possible.

And what was that? It was whatever had been previously unthinkable, if not impossible, thanks to the deadening hand of white male supremacy. Fullest scope and expression for non-whites: that was for starters. Next, fullest scope and expression for women. Then, the same for . . . for whatever someone (even a white male) found it edifying to express. Wait: maybe not "edifying." The word implies preference for one style over another style, one taste, one outlook, over something else. Hierarchy! Inequality! Gradations of value and worth! It was what the 1950s, of unblessed memory, would have affirmed. No, thanks. Instead of "edifying," say "satisfying." If a thing satisfied—forget old taboos and shibboleths—wasn't that enough?

As for religion, wasn't the nice God a decided improvement on the old God of Judgment, high in the heavens, thundering His displeasure with His creations, demanding from them reverence and obedience? Say your Christian flock hankers increasingly for the nice God. Do you not, supposing you minister to these lambs, feel tempted to bring on board at the very least the newer insights, the fresher ways of understanding what we mean by salvation?

The more we think of our common culture as a culture of general liberation, the better we comprehend the challenge inherent in ministry to it. A minister of the Gospel—Methodist, Presbyterian, Lutheran, Episcopalian—who comes bearing news of proper obligations finds himself under a serious burden. A culture of liberation wants no such news. It wants to know not what it can't or shouldn't do, but what it *can* do and, without further obstruction, *will* do. To that culture the minister says what, exactly? No? Yes? Maybe? The difficulties that lie in such a choice cannot and should not be underestimated.

What do I propose, then, as my course of action?

I am going to argue against many of the assumptions that my church, and like bodies of the Christian mainstream, have sopped up from the culture these past forty years, ostensibly for the sake of furthering Christian witness.

I am going to argue that these assumptions, far from strengthening Christian witness and potency, are likely keeping from the doors of our churches millions eager for an encounter with a God not presumed in advance to be merely "nice."

I am going to argue that, far from challenging secular styles and outlooks at odds with the Christian revelation, the churches have appropriated some of secularism's least rational notions—and thereby shamed themselves.

I will argue that the churches' love of such baubles, bought cheap in the marketplace, frequently outweighs their commitment to the Christians basics. And that this, in turn, makes them look like retailers not truth.

Another argument follows from that one. It is that our greatest mistake is in failing to see the Gospel as overriding mere circumstance and condition; conveying at all times and in all places, to all people, on equal terms, the same message of unconditional love and forgiveness. Our mistake, in other words, has been to overvalue cultural reflexes, to underestimate the power of the Christian Gospel to knock flat all divisions, all perspectives, by whomsoever adopted or concocted.

The Episcopal Church and the culture of the twenty-first century—by which I mean society's attitudes, tastes, preferences, and the like, as expressed in word and action—do not always by any means stroll hand in hand, whispering confidingly to each other. But their relationship, at least from the Episcopal side, has become intimate, self-reinforcing. The ways of the world have become, in frightening measure, the ways of the chameleon church still calling itself Episcopal.

The implications of the change in how Episcopalians "do" religion are impossible, at this early date, to understand fully. I argue all the same that we must begin to think about them, to handle and weigh them, holding them to the light, inspecting them up and down. What is this "religion" thing about anyway? Salvation, I believe, is the traditional answer: the merger of discrete human purposes with those of One whom the creeds identify as "Father Almighty, Maker of heaven and earth." Hanging around a church of traditional conviction, one gets the idea—at least one is supposed to—that such a God, nice or not, is highly consequential, more so than a television news anchor, a Hollywood studio head, a Nobel Prize laureate, a Fortune 500 executive, a bishop even.

Commonly, revolutions begin from below. Not the Episcopal revolution—a shake-up encouraged, sometimes imposed, from the top down. The apostles of cultural adaptation knew generally speaking what they wanted, hence what everyone else should want. While unconvinced Episcopaliansm in the '60s and afterwards, scratched their heads, wondering what was wrong with things that had so recently seemed right, those bent on effecting change informally, were organizing.

Again and again, in churchly councils, church "progressives" out-organized and outvoted the stodgy old standpatters—and from repeated successes gained confidence in the rightness of their endeavors. A "modernized" Book of Common Prayer, easily less cognizant of human sin than all its predecessor liturgies, went into the pews. New biblical teachings, sounding from the pulpit and the seminary lectern, raised new questions about the authenticity, hence the authority, of Scripture. Priesthood was bestowed for the first time on women, contrary to historic understandings of the priesthood's essentially "male" character. Outside the church, new moral attitudes took shape concerning the permanence and sacred nature of marriage. Rather quickly these attitudes made their way inside church walls. It became possible, then fashionable, then—for the aspiring—politically essential to challenge the idea that homosexuality was in the least troublesome or objectionable. Whence the authority for these and like assertions? The authority of the convinced seemed to suffice. They knew; they understood. They asserted no more than the culture asserted.

Decisive votes that went their way quickly turned the convinced into the arrogant. If an idea or a policy was good for them, it was good for everyone else. Bishops who advanced or supported the revolution either disciplined or ignored those dissenters who asked merely for space to be faithful to an older, and in their eyes holier, way. The tolerance on which Episcopalians once prided themselves had brought forth strange offspring—intolerance of the politically vanquished. This time, there would be no cutting off of heads. The cutting off of careers, and of associations and relationships, would suffice.

The consecration, in 2003, of Gene Robinson as the Episcopal Church's first avowed and practicing homosexual bishop focused international attention on conditions in the church and sped up an already steady exodus of laity and clergy. Dramatic (to put it as politely as possible) revision of the prayer book had driven away small numbers; larger numbers followed as the church undertook to ordain women. The increasingly speedy passage to affirmation of homosexuality cost the church many more members than had either of the earlier departures. Though, of course, the question is always open to dispute: How many depart for Reason X or for Reason Y? Or on account of spiritual fatigue? Or due to boredom or some other indefinable personal cause?

Even the Druids, it seems, are bailing out. While writing these lines, I happened on news that an East Coast Episcopal priest had renounced Christianity in order to become a full-time Druid, whereas before he had been just a part-time one, and mainly under cover. His wife was a Druid as well. I do not suggest such a priest is typical of Episcopal clergy. I suggest that the ability of our ecclesiastical environment to produce Druid priests may exceed like abilities in other, less (shall we say) freewheeling denominations.

Again I ask: Does it matter?

How can it not? What goes on in the modern Episcopal Church—what has gone on for the past four or five decades—bears on the affairs of all the mainstream churches, whose members are honorary children of the age in which they live, watching the same television shows and football games, eating the same fast foods, struggling with the same temptations, and constantly aware that the Christian consensus in the United States of America no longer exhibits the old signs of ruddy strength—aware, indeed, that the very need for Christianity seems to many, including some Christians, somehow smaller and more remote than formerly.

Let non-Episcopalians learn from us. We have been conducting an ecclesiastical estate sale: our godly heritage, our gift for worship and spirituality, priced for quick disposal on the marketplace. We're all in this thing together, in greater or lesser degree. But what thing is "this" thing? We can scarcely doubt, after the last forty years, the nature of the challenge. It is to present a very old faith to an age bent on reinventing itself—so it might seem—every few years, if not every few months.

Meanwhile—

THREE

We Few, We Happy Few

A BIT MORE ABOUT US, THEN, AS PREPARATION FOR WHAT follows: who we are, we Episcopalians, and how we got where we are—wherever that may be.

As the 1950s came and went, there was much to be said for us, that was for sure. Even non-Episcopalians sensed as much. Not that all delighted in contemplation of the Episcopal Church's vaunted specialness—its reputation for gentility; the richness and roll of the language that Episcopalians used to worship God; masonry churches smelling of history and ritual; social and economic prestige outsized for a membership easily smaller than that of the Methodists, Presbyterians, and Lutherans.

The Episcopal Church was the Church of England grafted into the American colonies, pruned and trimmed after the Revolution to suit changed circumstances but rooted still in the English Reformation of the sixteenth century. It was Protestant or Catholic—sometimes Protestant *and* Catholic—just as a parish (meaning a congregation) or a diocese (meaning a regional collection of parishes) desired.

In the church's formularies and traditions could be found warrant for biblical proclamation as the high point of Sunday worship, or, alternatively, for the Eucharistic feast of Christ's body and blood as the preferred emphasis (in which case "Holy Communion," as the name for the service, sometimes gave way to the Roman Catholic term "Mass"). There were "high" parishes and "low" parishes, terms that pertained to the parish's preference for preaching or sacramental celebration, sometimes just to a taste or distaste, as the case might be, for ceremonial detail and display. A "broad church" congregation (the term had more purchase in England than in the United States) was likelier to hear a particular Gospel passage construed as reproaching the social order—say, the capitalist environment—as opposed to rebuking the dark sins of heart and mind.

There was a certain messiness to the Episcopal way of life, as contrasted with the greater tidiness lived out in more single-minded bodies. Yet this same messiness rendered the church capable of attracting a broad range of worshippers, those who got past the persistent rumors of Episcopal snobbiness, or who took the sermon in whatever sense they preferred, finding in the Episcopal Church the perfect blend of *everything*. It was a Christian body with flair no less than commitment, comfortably—now and again, too comfortably—convinced of its sacred calling and plushy seat in the councils of the one, holy, catholic, and apostolic church.

Why such a church, nevertheless? Was it that God, some six hundred years ago—well into the Renaissance—conceived for his people in England a special witness which later was carried to the New World chiefly for the benefit of transplanted Englishmen?

The ways of the Almighty are famous for their lack of what could be called utter clarity. It seems clear at least that His Kingdom in England was faring well even as Henry Tudor, the eighth and most notorious of his name, ascended the throne in 1519. A part of popular wisdom is that Henry "founded" the Church of England so that he might divorce Catherine of Aragon and marry Anne Boleyn. Though he managed to achieve both marital goals, he founded nothing, ecclesiastically speaking. He merely (though it was not so "mere" a thing to his contemporaries) transferred headship of a thousand-year-old church from the Pope in far-off Rome to himself and his handpicked counselors and courtiers at Whitehall.

During Henry's lifetime—he died in 1547—the Church of England remained doctrinally and liturgically quite comparable to what it previously had been, with bishops, priests, and sacraments that closely tracked the Catholic understanding. Afterwards came significant Protestant accretions to faith and practice, and in worship the substitution of English ("a tongue understood of the people") for Latin. Such miseries and persecutions as Henry inflicted—for instance, expropriation of the monasteries and the execution of loyal and saintly Romanists like Sir Thomas More—had chiefly to do with the royal desire for revenues and for sheep-like obedience on his subjects' part. What had been the Church *in* England became the Church *of* England, the state church, of which to this day the sovereign remains nominal head.

When Englishmen reached the American colonies, less than a century after Henry's death, they brought with them, logically enough, the Church of England. At Jamestown, in 1607 (the occasion noted in the church's previously mentioned *New York Times* ad), a Church of England clergyman celebrated the Holy Communion under an awning, as Captain John Smith described it, made of sail, "til we cut planks, our pulpit a bar of wood nailed to two neighboring trees." It was a moment consonant with the evangelical style for which the church has never perhaps received full credit: resolute, unpretentious, not without significant effect.

Not every colony offered the church hospitality. The Puritans of New England wanted religious matters their own way, but the southern colonies, especially Virginia and South Carolina, embraced the church with some warmth, abandoning it only at the time of their Revolution, and then only with affectionate reluctance. Some Americans refused to give up either church or king. Of their number, many fled subsequently to a more welcoming Canada.

The end of the Revolution found the church in disarray and distress. Many of its clergy and laity had allied themselves with the crown; a number of these fled to Canada at war's end. Some who remained became objects of suspicion, as if membership in what had been the English church implied vestigial loyalty to England itself. Still, the remnant persisted, as remnants often will. Indeed, a noted Virginia Episcopalian, George Washington, would become the infant nation's first president.

Different local jurisdictions began referring to themselves as "the Protestant Episcopal Church," a convenient way of distinguishing themselves from the English church without puritanically renouncing the headship of bishops—*episcopi*. In fact, the "Episcopal" name was more pledge than reality. There were at the time no American bishops at all. Three Scottish bishops finally supplied this deficiency in 1784, consecrating the American Samuel Seabury for trans-Atlantic service. The Church of England consecrated two more Americans in 1786. Three years later, the new church's first General Convention drew up its own constitution and published its own Book of Common Prayer, shorn of prayers for the king but otherwise little altered in tone or language from the mother country's liturgy.

The new church was basically a confederation of dioceses, geographical units headed by bishops. Its prospects cannot have seemed especially sunny. With just one of every four hundred Americans claiming Episcopal affiliation, some energetic missionary work was clearly indicated. Some—indeed, much—energetic missionary work duly took place. A popular canard concerning Episcopalians has their missionaries arriving in frontier locations only after the railroads got there first. Stereotypes are notoriously hard to put down, but there is no historical warrant for the gibe that Episcopalians, as a body, were luxuriously indifferent to the hard calling of the missionary.

Great missionary bishops like Daniel Tuttle in the far West, Leonidas Polk in the South, and Alexander Garrett in Texas subjected themselves to inconveniences and dangers of every sort as they carried the Gospel to the rawest frontier settlements and outposts. When Helena, Montana, caught fire in 1869, Tuttle captained the firefighters—along with Gentle Joe, a gambler, and Bitter Root Bill, a "desperado." Polk, a West Point graduate and future Confederate general, whose notable North Carolina and Tennessee family included President James K. Polk, likened himself to a pioneer as he evangelized first Texas, then Louisiana.

Garrett came somewhat later than the others, but his quiet exploits have impressed me since, years ago, I first read his diaries. Whenever the frontier beckoned, which was regularly, he would hitch horse to buggy, bid his family goodbye, and journey forth from Dallas, on meager trails and sometimes through ferocious thunderstorms. Not infrequently he slept under the stars and celebrated Holy Communion on saloon tables. It was all by way of fulfilling the Episcopal calling. Still another great missionary bishop, Jackson Kemper, put the matter thus: "Possessing as we fully believe all those characteristics which distinguished the primitive [Church]:—A scriptural Liturgy—evangelical doctrines—and the apostolic succession—having the form of godliness and the power thereof—may it not be our duty to convert the world . . . !"

If Episcopalians were less outwardly fervent than, say, Methodists, it was largely because Episcopalianism, so to call it, was always a less fervent form of religious expression than others. Dignity and formality are among its enduring hallmarks; also a certain quietude, a particular dignity and self-restraint. It strikes me that one way of describing Episcopalians is as People Who Do Things in a Certain Way—the more so if those certain ways bear the imprint of ancient or just slightly mildewed practice. The Episcopal Church is a place for self-expression, but never in excess. *Please.*

The church in colonial times had marked itself out as the religious preserve of, to use an exceedingly broad and deceptive term, gentlemen. Gentlemen, as opposed to what? Peasants? Serfs? Not in the least. The church flung wide its doors. What many experienced on entering was, in purely democratic terms, not wholly inviting. First, a hushed and well-ordered worship space; then ceremony—words prayed from a book; music of a certain dignified solemnity; clergy arrayed in distinctly undemocratic-looking (and certainly foreign-appearing) garments that covered most of the body.

Yet the Episcopal Church's identification with property, education, and social position has some connection to reality. It was not unknown among Methodists in the 1950s (for such I was then) to pass among themselves, not hostile but less than well-pleased, remarks about the grandeur that Episcopalians supposedly imputed to themselves. An Episcopalian was known (quite aside from personal attributes, which often were delightful) for two things: enjoying a nip or two or three on social, and even non-social, occasions, and possessing means larger than most Methodists possessed.

In this there was much exaggeration, as in all characterizations of large human groupings. Certainly some social resentment was on display. The Episcopalians were good enough people. On the other hand, what made them such superior Christians, as Methodists, in peevish moods, sometimes put it? What was so wonderful about a book of written prayers, which happened to be essentially the same book from which John Wesley had adapted the Methodist Communion service?

Peter Taylor limned the perplexity in a short story, set in the middle of the twentieth century: "What a different breed [Episcopalians] had been from their Methodist and Presbyterian contemporaries. They danced and they played cards, of course, and they drank whiskey, and they did just about whatever they wanted on Sunday. . . . There were no graven images in the old church, but the Episcopalians had talked about the church as though it were the temple in Jerusalem itself. That was what their neighbors resented. Yes, they always spoke of it as '*the* Church,' as though there were no other church in town."

Whether by accident, intention, or an odd conjunction of both factors, the Episcopal Church oozed specialness. Here was not just *any* church. Here was one that presented, as Episcopalians saw it, a beguiling blend of all that was best in Christianity— orthodox doctrine; sacramental devotion balanced by devotion to Scripture; intellectual attainment; scholarship; architectural richness; liturgical know-how; good manners; good taste—and, with it all, intellectual spaciousness; willingness if not necessarily to *believe* a new story, or a new account, at least to hear, as a judge from his bench might hear an arresting new theory of contract law.

Where was the harm in hearing, after all? Some new insight might emerge, some new way of understanding old problems and challenges. In the Episcopal Church no book could be presumed closed. Narrowness of outlook was frowned upon. Narrowness implied both sterility and finality, neither one acceptable

51

to Christians. The globe on which we lived was ever spinning, ever dying, ever renewing itself. A good way to become irrelevant—except possibly for tourist purposes, such as the Old Order Amish served, with their beards and buggies—was to pretend that whatever needed to be known *was* known. But who was likely to listen long as you argued to this effect?

A distinguished, certainly orthodox, twentieth-century archbishop of Canterbury, Michael Ramsey, spoke for many when he noted: "Under the guidance of the Holy Spirit we are given fresh understandings and fresh articulation of what has been revealed originally in all kinds of hidden seeds." Anglicans—Episcopalians—waited expectantly for those seeds to germinate. Meanwhile, tall brass processional crosses led the way to the Altar, where all such questions could be laid with pious expectancy. All would in due course be revealed. The church abided that moment.

It was never, of course, as good as all that. Of no institution, no human grouping or coalition whatever, anywhere, may it be said that ideals and practice are as one. That is not the way of the world. I leave the reader to point out, if he likes, any notable exceptions to that assertion. Unless we are to tarry, I need to mention those special ways in which the Episcopal Church fell short of that specialness to which Episcopal theorists sometimes pretended.

There was first the whole elite aura of the church, its social as well as ecclesiastical propriety. If the Episcopal Church was never really the Church of the Rich, still it welcomed a very large number of the rich, people who endowed it with their own way of looking at life. Clarence Day, Sr., of *Life with Father* fame, had in the Gilded Age embraced the Episcopal Church as "a church [so Day Jr. wrote] managed like a department of a gentleman's Government. He liked such a church's strong Tory flavor, and its recognition of castes. He liked its "deference to sound, able persons who knew how to run things, and its confidence in their integrity and right point of view."

The Vanderbilts, Astors, and Whitneys were among those sound, able persons, as was Franklin Delano Roosevelt—as was John Pierpont Morgan, who, according to Kit and Frederica Konolige, saw the Episcopal Church as "another agency for the improvement of America and the American aristocracy." By the 1950s, reported Vance Packard, corporation executives were ten times as likely as other Americans to identify themselves as Episcopalians; furthermore, three-quarters of social weddings reported in the *New York Times* took place in Episcopal churches.

What of it, aside from the potential for class snobbery and reactionary defense of privilege? The question is plausible: little more than that. Superficial acquaintance with nineteenth-century novels could give the impression of a moat between rich and poor, dug and maintained by the rich for their exclusive benefit, impassable except in tales where the factory owner's son weds the daughter of the head housekeeper or some such. It would be more to the point to note how impermanent is "class" identity in America, given the constant migration upwards and downwards between various classes—the general direction nonetheless being upward—with so-called social lines marked as often by automobiles as by attitudes.

Even more to the present point is a reality of our own times: wealthier Americans as the main source *challenging*, rather than defending, status quos of every description, working to tear down whatever they see as privilege conditioned on race, sex, or money. A much-remarked irony of modern life is that the prosperous and educated—the basic Episcopal constituency—make up the country's most "progressive," or liberal, social bloc, with many seeming to feel a special entitlement or obligation to shove others, ready or not, along the supposed upward path. ("Why?" is a question best reserved for another place, given the complexities always involved in assigning motive.)

White college students, especially at prestigious institutions like Yale and Berkeley, were deeply involved in the social upheavals of the 1960s. Today, in the seats of worldly power—educational, political, cultural, and religious—many of these former rebels sit confidently. That may partly explain the relationship between the elite and the cultural left. Shelby Steele, the distinguished black scholar, ventures a complementary interpretation: "White guilt" as motive behind the unwillingness of white leaders to enforce moral norms that might be seen as vestiges of the white supremacy era. Enough. Let us go on.

A few words about another Episcopal hallmark, our relaxed and spacious tradition of "tolerance." The tradition flows from the habit, described previously, of listening, if only from politeness, to different viewpoints. It was long the manner of the Episcopalian, and of his church, to seek in most matters—not excluding theological matters—a middle way between extremes. The middle way might not be suited to the ultimate resolution of deeply vexed questions; still, it kept oxen out of the ditches on either side of the path. And, with luck, not to mention grace, the whole thing might be counted on to blow over. A problem deferred was in some complicated sense a problem solved. Never to say more than necessary under the circumstances, never to look anxiously at detail when a more general examination got the job done—here were eminently Episcopal traits. I see these traits as proceeding from a couple of cultural factors.

First, the factor of *class*. Something of the establishment lawyer's cast of mind permeates Episcopalianism. That might be because so many establishment lawyers have for so long peopled so many Episcopal pews. Or it might not be. I would not rule out all the same, as a factor in Episcopal caution, the inherent caution of the financial elite, wishing not to throw away hard-won advantage or to unduly increase exposure to risk. A competent attorney advises his client of the best way not to get into trouble but to stay out of it. With new money the instinct is different: It is to risk and dare and stick out the neck. The point worth emphasizing here, at the risk of over-simplifying, is that old money strongly influenced the old Episcopal Church—old money determined to get still older.

A second factor grows from even deeper Episcopal soil: the factor of *Englishness*. Englishness is no surprise in the Church of England or in that church's offspring; especially what could be miscalled the "Anglo-Saxon" world—the United States, Canada, Australia, New Zealand, and the English communities of South Africa. English DNA is in all the works and viewpoints of the Episcopal Church in the United States of America. The resistance of some American Anglicans to the American Revolution was founded on their strong attachment to English ways.

So what is particularly "English" about the Episcopal Church? First, its membership. Moving from east to west, the Episcopal Church scooped up with special ease large quantities of members with English names—Smith, Jones, Black, Carter, Townsend, Gilman, Harrison. I confess to generalizing. A glance through a recent clergy directory makes it clear that we have Meierses, Cesars, and Gonzalezes—just not in nearly the same quantity.

"Englishness" means, then, that Episcopalians have "been here" longer than many others have been. It implies the incorporation of English experience into life and worship; a taste for Wordsworth, Austen, and C. S. Lewis, and certainly for the cadences and rhythms of the Book of Common Prayer; a fondness for visiting and worshipping amid the ancient stones of English churches, and for drinking in thirstily the rich polyphony of Thomas Tallis and William Byrd as it pours from the white-ruffed throats of young choristers.

Englishness, in a purely theological context, further implies caution. Religion (as Episcopalians have always seen it) is clearly a Good Thing, but specifics of doctrine and viewpoint are not to be pressed too hard or impolitely. There had been more of this sort of thing on the Continent, during the Reformation, but there had been enough in England, from Henry VIII's time until Oliver Cromwell's, to excite a distrust or fear of religious firmness. Henry had burned Catholics; his older daughter, Mary, had ignited Protestants. His younger daughter, Elizabeth, had sought religious peace, in part through the blurring of religious differences.

A taste for pushing things farther and harder than was quite prudent showed up in the Stuarts; the second Stuart king, Charles I, lost his throne and his head over it. Oliver Cromwell, the Protector, and the major generals he used to govern the country, rammed ultra-Protestantism as far down English throats as they possibly could. Succeeding rulers were more careful about pressing for unanimity of viewpoint and practice. A similar disposition came to dominate the practice of the Episcopal Church. Gentlemen might fight when obliged to, but they hoped to be spared the necessity. Settling things without rancor was so much more gracious, so much more *civilized*.

Or so it seemed.

FOUR

We Shall Overcome

FEW WOULD STARE WITH WILD SURMISE IF FUTURE HISTORIANS should declare the civil rights revolution the central event of the American twentieth century, the occasion that knocked askew the underpinnings of an older order and overthrew familiar standards of judgment and action.

The serious business of equalizing the moral scales goes persistently forward in the present century. Not that (as well we know!) the passage of four decades has rendered all the many races one, in heart as in mind. The point is that, due to the civil rights revolution, a whole array of assumptions—some of them cruel, some prudent and generous, some indifferent in any moral sense—would receive no serious hearing today were they to be raised publicly (a highly unlikely prospect, by the way).

The civil rights revolution awakened spirits that would not be quieted. They hovered and flitted over the landscape, whispering not just that Jim Crow's demise had been too long delayed but that society's methods for measuring justice and dignity needed amendment, if not outright replacement. Replacement with what? In the 1960s, you never could tell. With whatever an orator or demonstrator—battalions, regiments, armies of both were on call—might happen to claim. The civil rights revolution inspired in no small degree the duly noted frenzies of that decade. Hardly a one of us, as the 1950s faded, could have foretold such cultural disruptions as lay ahead for the nation, and for the world.

There they were anyway. Something had to be made of them, not least by the visible representatives of Jesus Christ: bishops, priests, clergy, theologians of all faiths and stripes. To such large events as these the churches simply had to speak. They had first, naturally, to decide what they would say.

The end of the Second World War had left the United States contemplating strenuously, for the first time in decades, the racial relationships it had improvised to account for emancipation in 1865 and the demand for post-Civil War reconciliation between North and South. The war of 1941–1945 had been waged against regimes that embraced truly toxic notions of racial superiority. With the war's end, sympathy for blacks began to accumulate, then consolidate. Early signs of change were as impressive as they were scattered: the Brooklyn Dodgers' hiring of Jackie Robinson; Hollywood's discovery that not all blacks were Pullman porters or maids, and that some making up, in non-comical cinematic portrayals of blacks, might be due for the country's neglect of a whole class of its citizens; President Harry Truman's order to end segregation in the armed forces; federal court decisions gradually prying open the doors of law schools closed to blacks.

In 1954 came the U.S. Supreme Court's unanimous finding, in *Brown* v. *Board of Education*, that segregation in public schools violated the Constitution. The civil rights era had well and truly begun. Its narrative line is so familiar by now, I trust, as not to warrant rehearsing here. I would speak only of the Episcopal

Church's identification with the struggle—a kind of mold-breaking identification whereby the church, having decided on aggressive support of a secular cause, found the satisfactions of that struggle increasingly central to its self-concept.

"Secular cause?" It was that, all right, and it was more. Were not blacks the creations, hence the children, of God? Was not salvation through Jesus Christ available to them on the same terms as to whites and everyone else? If so, and it was certainly so, religious solidarity with their cause was a clear necessity. Yet the battlegrounds in this titanic contest were for the most part secular: courtrooms, jail cells, legislative corridors, places where the U.S. Constitution and the Gettysburg Address were more likely to be quoted extensively than the Four Gospels or the Creeds, not to mention the Book of Common Prayer.

The Episcopal Church's new self-understanding, as it emerged in the 1960s and unfolded thereafter, rested on the perception that the time had come for prophetic engagement with secular society: especially the society of the South, where the largest number of black Americans lived, and where secular enactments divided them personally, as well as residentially, from whites. No longer would the church automatically affirm, or appear to, the undertakings of that society. If anything, it would challenge those undertakings.

The evolving identity of the church appeared to answer the critiques of the 1950s. No engagement with society? No effort, in Peter Berger's words, to "modify the social structure itself?" Not any longer. Here was a church beginning to stir itself at last. To many, including Episcopalians, the Episcopal Church seemed not that kind of church. It was more a social clique, more disposed to stand apart from other people's business than to meddle in it.

For all that, much of the membership and leadership of the Episcopal Church—note the qualifying adjective "much"—

embraced with generosity and dedication the coming of the civil rights revolution. This was due, as is ever the case with vast movements, to a vast number of reasons and motives. By the standards of the mid-twentieth century, the Episcopal Church's record on race relations was far from paltry or contemptible. Episcopal missionaries, in antebellum times, had baptized slaves, incorporating them fully, perhaps even a little daringly, into the church. There arose in due course a black Episcopal elite that at one time included Cab Calloway, Nat King Cole, and the civil rights attorney and future Supreme Court justice Thurgood Marshall. If the church had not pushed aggressively for civil rights, well, neither had most other religious or political assemblages. White Episcopalians, particularly in the segregated South, were likelier to employ than to mingle or compete with blacks, including black Episcopalians who attended "their own" churches, rather than whites ones.

Gradually the theological implications of the struggle for racial justice gained the upper hand over secular ones (e.g., federal interference in local matters as an unhealthy and dangerous precedent). Dr. Martin Luther King, Jr., a Baptist minister whose name recalls both the Reformation and the Holy Scriptures, endowed the civil rights movement with religious fervor and orientation, preaching equality as a Gospel obligation. Northern Episcopalians early entered the civil rights lists, often tilting with their own brethren in the Southern parishes and dioceses, who pleaded for *patience* as they addressed, with varying degrees of enthusiasm, the new order of things.

Significant passion was abroad in the church, if not in every nave or pew. Consider the kind of simmering dissatisfaction that already existed in the 1950s, the gnawing apprehension that the church was neglecting its duty to the urban wilderness. That duty, as particular Episcopalians elucidated it, was simply to minister, to bind up and where possible to heal, and if nothing else, just to stand in solidarity with the suffering.

"The Church," wrote the Episcopal layman William String-fellow, "must trust the Gospel enough to come among the poor with nothing to offer the poor except the Gospel." Stringfellow went further yet. Taking his own advice, he moved to East Harlem—a Harvard-educated lawyer living amid "the smells of sweat and waste, bathtubs in the kitchens, antiquated direct current, predatory vermin, second-hand clothes, and a million empty beer cans in the gutters"—in order to provide the poor with legal services otherwise unavailable to them. In his widely read and cited writings he continued to challenge his church with the duty of promoting social justice, of uprooting the "idolatry of race." "[H]ow woefully," he lamented, "the churches have underestimated the gravity and vehemence and passion of the racial crisis in America."

Another white Episcopalian whose ear caught the sound of the trumpet was Sarah Patton Boyle, a University of Virginia faculty wife. In 1950, she felt led to support the suit of a young black man, Gregory Swanson, for admission to the University's law school. It was on from there to the outspoken, if decorous, advocacy she would chronicle in her memoir of a decade later, *The Desegregated Heart: A Virginian's Stand in Time of Transition.* Sarah Boyle was one of few white women to join the National Association for the Advancement of Colored People. The sight of a cross burned on her lawn, presumably by white supremacists, was, in her eyes, a "a blaze of loveliness formed in the symbol of eternal love."

Where the impromptu leadership had ventured, the ordained leadership began in due course to follow, putting in a word, and often more than a word, for the goals of the civil rights movement. Said one bishop: "Our immediate task is to establish as rapidly as is humanly possible and as widely as is human possible, equality of opportunity for *all* the people of our land." When, in 1955, Houston, the designated host city for the church's General Convention, could not or would not guarantee nonsegregated accommodations, church officials moved the convention to Honolulu. There the deputies pronounced segregation "contrary to the mind of Christ and the will of God." With Martin Luther King and his followers pushing for all they were worth against the regime of segregation, the presiding bishop of the Episcopal Church declared it "a cause of rejoicing to the Christian community that black Americans—and oppressed peoples everywhere—are displaying a heightened sense of human dignity in their refusal to accept second-class citizenship any longer."

In 1963, ten Episcopal bishops and some three hundred priests and deacons accompanied King—and, so it seemed, half of America—on the greatest civil rights march of all, to the Lincoln Memorial in Washington, D.C., where the great civil rights leader communicated unforgettably his dream of racial unity and brotherhood.

Not that Southern Episcopalians rejoiced as one to hear even from fellow Episcopalians that that their social mores were at best outmoded, at worst downright wicked. The godly and much-loved bishop of Alabama, Charles Colcock Jones Carpenter, pronounced King's Selma-to-Montgomery march "a foolish business and sad waste of time."

Whereas today, despite the achievements of his ministry, relatively few Episcopalians can recall Carpenter's name, the Episcopal Church honors as a martyr the young Northern seminarian who was murdered in Lowndes County, Alabama, in that same tumultuous year of 1965. Jonathan Daniels, answering the call, as he described it, of "living theology," had marched from Selma to Montgomery. He also had made the integration of St. Paul's Episcopal Church, Selma, a personal cause, to the vexation of a rector trapped, like many a centrist before and since, between angry polarities of viewpoint. In 1991, the Episcopal Church enrolled Daniels's name in its Calendar of Lesser Feasts and Fasts. "O God of justice and compassion," reads the collect appointed for the day commemorating his murder by shotgun, " . . . We give thee thanks for thy faithful witness, Jonathan Myrick Daniels . . . and we pray that we, following his example, may make no peace with oppression."

It was no small witness that the Episcopal Church, like the society of which it was a part, had compiled quickly, earnestly, on behalf of civil rights. Nor was it a witness lightly to be put aside, despite the perhaps inevitable disillusionments that followed swiftly. Not a few well-intentioned whites who had given the civil rights cause crucial and timely backing in the early 1960s woke up later in the decade to find their beneficiaries kicking them around. Among those rubbing startled eyes were some of the same Episcopalians who had supposed, not unreasonably, that years of earnest marching and praying had earned them a measure of—well, perhaps *gratitude*?

The rise of the black power movement destroyed any such facile hopes. Anger was, so to speak, all the rage. While gangs of college students and campus hangers-on sought (among many other things) to procure an American exit from Vietnam, inner-city gangs set their own neighborhoods ablaze in cities from Newark, New Jersey, to Los Angeles, California. The Mark Antony of Shakespeare's *Julius Caesar* seemed to have anticipated everything: "O judgment, thou art fled to brutish beasts/And men have lost their reason!"

As for suitably enlightened Episcopalians and their ilk, what did they want, anyway, medals for belated performance of duty? Dr. Martin Luther King's 1968 assassination cleared the way for a different style of leader—angrier, more bellicose, less inclined to join hands as though grouped around a church campfire, listening to the plink of guitars.

The story of the Episcopal Church's disastrous encounter with the black power movement need not detain us long, though it can be said to have driven the first wedge between the more conservative sort of Episcopalian and his now conspicuously liberal leaders. A new presiding bishop of the church, John Hines, a Southerner deeply committed to civil rights, declared, "We are part of the problem inasmuch as the sickness of our society is our sickness also." There was possibly something to be said for that assessment, just as a matter of logic, but the 1960s was not a period for quiet contemplation of intellectual constructs. Black "militants" (to use the terminology of that day), inside and especially outside the Episcopal Church, were clamoring for economic "reparations" and financial grants. Bloody inner-city riots in 1967 had hinted at one alternative. It might have been centuries since the Montgomery bus boycott; it was, in fact, just eight years. An evil genius seemed to stalk the land, turning American against American.

The General Convention Social Program (GCSP), adopted at the General Convention of 1967, was an attempt partially to reorient the church as a factor in the healing of social ills—to support, as Hines put it, "the dispossessed and oppressed people of this country." The GCSP, Hines promised, "will encourage the use of political and economic power to support justice and self-determination for all men." That meant, in practical terms, annual grants of $3 million from Episcopal resources to empower the poor, help root out society's racism, and generally "support justice and self-determination for the poor and powerless."

What was "justice"? Poverty and powerlessness were definable—how? There was no time, or anyway scant time had been made, for the consideration of these and like matters. At a moment of crisis, Episcopalians were destined to learn on the fly. The GCSP, an ill-digested farrago of assumptions about society's needs and the ability of the Christian church to address them, went badly almost from the start. That is to say, it attracted immediate attention on account of grants it made to controversial recipients, such as a Hispanic organization—whose leader was in jail—that sought to force the return of the American Southwest to Hispanic control!

Subventions of this sort more than made the Episcopal Church look ridiculous; they angered Episcopalians who felt that they were putting up with plenty of social revolution as it was without having to fund it, too. When, in 1969, a special convention voted $200,000 for reparations to minorities, many Episcopalians sensed that some theological Rubicon was about to be crossed, with the church assuming the role of packhorse for the wrathful and disreputable. It never came quite to that. Dazed, the church paused in midstream and rethought its undertakings. The 1970 General Convention adopted a process designed to make sure grants went only to generally worthy causes, whatever that might mean. Soon enough, a nation shocked at the fatal shootings of four Kent State University students by National Guardsmen suppressing an antiwar protest gasped out a plea for calm. Civil rights protest waned, though the U.S. government continued energetically to prosecute racial segregation. Life grew slightly less tumultuous and for just a while—hardly less in the sacred precincts of the Episcopal Church than elsewhere.

But nothing would ever be the same again. The 1960s had unsettled the whole of society. There was no recapturing the vapors that filled the air. Nor did the Episcopal Church seem desirous of trying.

The struggle for civil rights had brought the Episcopal Church to a new way of thinking about its role in society and its criteria for action.

If the 1960s had a theme, it was liberation: the disentanglement of individuals from old obligations, either illegitimate (officially enforced discrimination) or, as it often fell out, legitimate (dress, manners, family relationships). It proved not always easy in practice to explain the difference. The 1960s had accustomed Americans to the exercise of autonomy and choice. A choice was a choice, was it not? And choice was to be protected. Manifestly that was so with civil rights. To oppose laws and regulations and customs that barred blacks from particular venues was to assert the right of these same blacks to the dignity of choice—the same dignity that whites enjoyed without legal hindrance. The nation saw blacks as citizens entitled under the Constitution to the rights of all citizens, irrespective of race. The churches—conspicuously including, as we have seen, the Episcopal Church—pushed the matter further still. The constitutional argument was correct, but blacks were children of God every bit as much as they were citizens of the United States, perhaps more so. It was Christianity's clear duty to recognize them as such and to insist on their full incorporation into the Christian commonwealth, "the blessed company of all faithful people," as the Book of Common Prayer, with customary eloquence, phrased the matter.

The Episcopal Church had risked much, dared much, to stand alongside blacks asserting their civil rights. Now just who else was out there, similarly disenfranchised? What other segments of society needed help of the same kind the church had been pleased and proud to extend blacks, both within and without the church? The matter was subjective in large degree. No other social segments toiled under quite the same disadvantages as blacks had for so long: that is to say, the disadvantage conferred by an external factor. That factor, of course, was skin color, or, to put it another way, descent from African slaves brought in chains to these shores and made to labor without their consent. There were other externals besides race, however. It remained to assess them and determine to what degree, if any, they had invited oppression and degradation.

The clearest of these was sex. Or so various Americans began to assert, at just about the time (circa 1970) that general acknowledgment of black Americans' rights was becoming reality instead of dream. The idea of women as a similarly, or comparably, oppressed class was in no way new. Particular women had argued for, worked for, agitated for, rights equal to those enjoyed by their fathers, husbands, and brothers. The cause of "liberating" women—mostly in abeyance since male society gave female society the vote in the early twentieth century—came to fascinate Americans in the 1970s, not least on account of certain resemblances to the civil rights cause which women were glad enough to point out.

In due course, women gained more tangible freedoms than they or the menfolk, either one, might have imagined possible just twenty or thirty years earlier. Churches participated enthusiastically in the new crusade. As early as 1970, the Episcopal Church admitted women to ordained ministry and went on from there to affirm them in the highest positions of leadership. We shall soon see how all this came to pass.

Even with the liberation of women, the spirit of liberation remained unappeased, unsatisfied. Other asserted rights cried out for fulfillment—rights that society, and much of its Christian component, sought where possible to gratify. There was some commonality here with the push for women's liberation, in that women—some, by no means all—had sought the kind of sexual autonomy they saw men as enjoying. Sex without shame was more or less the slogan, though I can recall no one's expressing it in those precise terms. Sex was part of personhood. To regulate it went against—well, what? The right to bodily expression. The right to emotional fulfillment. These rights were written down nowhere in common law or the moral code, yet they have come in our own time to obsess advanced thinkers. The abortion of a pregnancy is one such "expression" to gain official sanction in the past few decades. Homosexuality possibly treads the same path to acceptance. One cannot yet be sure. One *can* be sure that desire alone has come in our time to assume almost unassailable status in the social order.

The right to desire: How are we to forbid it? On what grounds? Religious grounds would once have sufficed. Not all desires were good or worthy, according to the Christian revelation. Not all are good even now, but a larger number are made to seem good than ever before was the case. Whether or not we would dream of forbidding certain things our forefathers forbade, we would not likely try now, knowing or suspecting our inability to get away with it. We simply shrug more than formerly, there being infinitely more "rights".

There is one more sense in which the Episcopal Church's civil rights experience became the pivot on which future thought and action would swing. The social policy, as it were, of Holy Scripture had come under blistering attack. As in the years before the Civil War, so in the 1960s and 1970s: The Bible's seeming acceptance of the master-slave relationship made the Good Book something less than a reliable guide to newer mores and the enlivened understandings that God's people had acquired since the first century A.D. Many antebellum American Christians had resorted to biblical "proofs" for the naturalness of slavery, citing, for instance, Noah's curse on Ham (Genesis 8:24–27), the putative ancestor of the Africans.

From the Flood to a New Orleans slave block—a huge and highly questionable stretch indeed! Nor did it hide from view God's decisive part in the largest act of emancipation prior to Mr. Lincoln, the loosing of the Hebrew slaves from Egyptian bondage. A determined Christian with time on his hands could find in the Bible evidence of divine warrant for no end of notions. Or, alternatively, evidence to confute such notions . It was hardly the fault of the Bible or its most woolly-minded translators. In a sense, it was perverse testimony to the truth of a New Testament exhortation: "Seek and ye shall find."

The salient point, for what lay ahead in Christian and Episcopal history, was that the civil rights crusade intensified a habit growing already in theological circles—that of regarding the Bible's prescriptions, and those of historic Christian theology, as subject to challenge and change as modern awarenesses blossomed like autumn roses.

Secular society was certainly acquiring the habit. In *Brown v. Board of Education*, the U.S. Supreme Court had overruled, as inconsistent with evolved moral understandings, its own 1896 precedent (*Plessy v. Ferguson*) allowing "separate but equal" accommodation of blacks in public places, such as schools. The principle now to be accommodated under the Constitution was that of racial equality. If learned judges had in the past argued otherwise, that was too bad. We knew better now. We would apply our own understandings, not those of previous interpreters.

There was a certain subjectivity to the enterprise: "Our" view wiser than "their" view, more in keeping with evolved habits of thought. One recognized here a cultural factor of profound importance—the tendency to supplant older understandings of texts and principles with supposedly clearer, cleaner ones, rooted to some extent in the appreciation of evolution as the motive power in human affairs. We were not the same as those slope-browed, club-carrying, supposed forbears of ours, were we? Well, then, onward and upward! Let the dead bury the dead! It was the rude, abrasive spirit of the French Revolution, refracted through the hearty progressivism of American life, all the more compelling in a culture seemingly determined to rewrite everything we thought we knew of life.

As we have noted, modern Anglicanism might, and did, profess deep respect for Christian tradition and for Scripture, but more often than not with fingers decorously crossed. The past was not everything, was it? Nor was the great book of Christianity just a dry text. It dripped instead with life, and life was movement, change, evolution. The Spirit could be counted on to gratify new generations with new knowledge and understandings. Wrote Bishop Frederick Borsch of Los Angeles: "The Bible is not meant to be a written code that kills but a vehicle of the Spirit that gives life."

And how were we to know what the Spirit was saying to us? Here the matter got tricky. "Experience" and "reason" were the attributes that Episcopal voices commended most often. "Reason," that is, the activity of the mind, was one of the three legs holding up the familiar stool of Anglican authority, along with Scripture and Tradition. Of course the stool itself, however impressive to look at, lacked formal standing. No Episcopal formularies required belief in it. It was a way of thinking. There might be other ways. Sure enough, the more restless sort of Episcopalian, joined by restless types in the other mainline Christian churches, began invoking Experience, as embodying the manner in which the church had lived and worked through quotidian situations. Among those situations was that of cruelty and indifference toward black Americans.

In another mood, Americans might have let it go with appropriating this valuable new understanding, declining to think of

Scripture as a cultural and sociological trap for moderns, a depository for archaic attitudes in need of scrubbing up or discarding altogether. When the Episcopal Church came to consider the place and role of Episcopal women, it recalled that certain "old" attitudes about blacks, supposedly "approved" by Scripture, had turned out wrong or wrong-headed. What about women? Wasn't it possible—likely, even—that all this time parchment prescriptions had blinded everyone, most women included, to the truth and justice of womanhood's claims to fulfillment? Let such prescriptions go! So also those blinding us to the rightful claims of gay people! From the previous step, female emancipation, gay emancipation followed ineluctably for the church, once it became clear to many that much of all we thought we knew was snare and delusion. It remained only to move on, to do the right thing, to atone for the injustices of the past.

The civil rights movement first gave the Episcopal Church the feel for casting over the side, into the water, heavy historical weights seen as no longer useful, weights that tied down thought and action. That very little indeed should be thus bound is the study of the present-day Episcopal Church, which in extraordinary degree identifies its own causes with those of the secular, material culture. Whatever the culture supports—at least those cultural elements congenial to Episcopalians—the Church regularly finds itself supporting and promoting, gay rights being only the latest case study. It is as though this great Christian body, admiring the culture's vivacity, had deliberately sat down alongside the exemplars of that culture, hoping to draw from them warmth and purpose.

The time has come to see how the Episcopal Church's chameleon instincts, like similar instincts visible to members of the other mainline churches, are presently manifesting themselves, and with what consequences. That is where we go now, toward understanding what Episcopalians have been up to since the civil rights era, and toward discerning, if we can, whether all that it has been up to can be squared in any meaningful sense with the things Christians have said about their religion since—well, since always and forever.

FIVE
Lord Have Mercy upon Us

IRST, THOUGH, THERE WAS INTERNAL BUSINESS TO ACCOMPLISH—
some housecleaning, some tidying up. There was a momentousness about the enterprise that has attracted too little attention from analysts of "the Episcopal crisis." The process of prayer book revision, carried out mostly after civil rights tumult and shouting had died away, reshaped the Episcopal Church in ways too little grasped at the time. Like the church's civil rights involvement, prayer book revision steered Episcopalians—decisively—toward new patterns of life and thought. We need to talk of how this came to be. And why.

A new age had arrived. . Living and acting and witnessing in such an age seemed to require a new way of conversing with the Lord and showing forth His works and words. So at least the church's core leadership, as distinguished from its membership at large, had become powerfully convinced. The ensuing tussle over revision of the historic Book of Common Prayer revealed, astoundingly, which way the wind had begun blowing in Episcopal affairs and how resolute the church's leaders had become in pursuit of a new course.

For four centuries the Book of Common Prayer had been the worship text of Anglicans the world around, revised occasionally according to local needs and changed perspectives. Never was it changed without care, caution, and a certain civilized regret. Well into the 1960s, the Book of Common Prayer, as adapted by the Episcopal Church for its own use, was in all important particulars the same book of services that the Church of England had promulgated following Henry VIII's break with the Pope.

The prayer book, in a context flightier than holy places usually afford, could be called Anglicanism's signature tune. The words that Anglicans for centuries spoke to God, as framed chiefly through the genius of Thomas Cranmer, Henry's Archbishop of Canterbury, have often been likened to music—music of the highest order, not only presenting Christian truth (as understood by Anglicans) but also capable, on the right occasions, of lifting souls to heaven. This same music would become, out of the recognition and familiarity that accompany acknowledged accomplishment, an unofficial part of American Protestantism's regular worship. That was because in prayer book language there was a resonance not always to be had in ecclesiastical prose. It found its way to the innermost places of the soul. As a *Washington Post* book critic noted not long ago, in tribute, "The simple beauty of the prayer book's prose, especially in its collects [prayers that 'collect' the congregation's petitions for particular days and occasions], displays perfect pitch for sound and rhythmical balance."

Over time, prayer book phrases of every sort embedded themselves in public consciousness: "the devil, the world, and the flesh"; "Wilt thou have this woman to thy wedded wife?"; "To have and to hold from this day forward, for better for worse, for richer for poorer." In still another setting: "earth to earth, ashes to ashes, dust to dust, in sure and certain hope of the Resurrection to eternal life." It was the language of human beginnings and endings. Also of hope and humility: "Lighten our darkness, we beseech thee, O Lord"; "We have erred and strayed from thy ways like lost sheep,/We have followed too much the devices and desires of our own hearts."

Miles Coverdale's no less musical translation of the Psalter, a feature of the prayer book from the start, burrowed no less deeply into the soul: "God is our hope and strength: a very present help in trouble"; "Thou shalt not be afraid for any terror by night, nor for the arrow that flieth by day"; "The Lord is my light and my salvation."

Language of this strength and excellence worked gently to rein in human egos, to the extent, anyway, that anything can be credited with reining in the human ego! Given that, as Coverdale's Psalter spaciously put it, "the earth is the Lord's and the fulness thereof," clearly the Lord exceeded in all respects those who knew themselves to be—again, the Psalter—"the people of his pasture, and the sheep of his hand."

The prayer book could be unashamedly direct in rebuking human pretension. "[B]ecause the frailty of man without thee cannot but fall," one collect acknowledged without shame or regret. Another collect besought God to "grant . . . that we, who cannot do anything that is good without thee, may by thee be enabled to live according to thy will." All this was good Christian theology, slightly tinged with the Calvinism of the Reformation. It was, more to the present point, Christian theology of an especially emphatic sort, poured week after week into the mind of the Anglican worshipper, to the degree that said worshipper sat or knelt with mind open.

If Anglicanism lacked strong methods for enforcement of the Anglican viewpoint—in Anglican affairs, the archbishop of Canterbury is more figurehead than authority figure—the rhetoric of prayer helped fill the gap: There was "no health in us." "Through the weakness of our mortal nature" we could "do no good thing" without God. And so on: every page, every phrase, bespeaking in some way the hopelessly, wondrously unchallengeable power of God and the puniness, by comparison, of His creations. Language and belief of this kind were headed for collision with whatever culture might decide in the future that stringency spoiled the human broth, unreasonably compromising individual choice and perception.

Not all Anglicans probably ever believed of themselves and each other all that the prayer book declared or implied. Katherine Hepburn's character in the 1932 movie, "A Bill of Divorcement," dismissed an English prayer book petition for "miserable sinners." "I'm not 'miserable,'" she declared loftily, "and I'm not a 'sinner'!" Still, the theological markers were there for viewing whenever required: tall, strong, and splendidly crafted.

No other Christian body, it seems safe to say, has ever surpassed, liturgically speaking, the Anglicans. The prayer book constantly reinforced Anglicanism's appeal to a certain type of worshipper. If it was signature tune, so also was it secret weapon, capable of penetrating the sensibility of seekers who, hearing the wonderful words, desired to hear them again and again. The prayer book took hold on first acquaintance. It pulled and tugged with uncanny power. The Baptists never spoke so, nor the Presbyterians, nor the Campbellites. The Roman Catholics worshipped in stilted, frequently incomprehensible Latin. The Episcopalians were the ones with perfect liturgical pitch. Such prayers as they raised were bound to reach, yes—without static or interruption—the very throne of God.

Well, one might say, if all this was true, why mess around with such a decided asset to the faith? The enterprise went, to a degree, against instinct and also good counsel: "If it ain't broke, don't fix it." Was the prayer book "broke," nevertheless? In the 1950s and 1960s, no small number of Episcopalians were asking just that question—and answering in the affirmative. If not "broke," according to the normal usage of the word, the Book of Common Prayer seemed to some Episcopalians a candidate for significant repairs. There were various complaints, with a decidedly cultural edge.

Like virtually all Christians at the time (save the Catholics, of course), influenced as they were by the dominant style of the King James Version, Episcopalians said "thee" and "thou" to the Lord, and "wast" and "art" and "shalt." But who, save in church, talked that way anymore? The church was making its message quaint and obscure by framing it in sixteenth-century language. Or so one began hearing and reading if one was attuned to nice questions of propriety and effectiveness in worship. Had it not been a major goal of the English Reformers in the sixteenth century to substitute for liturgical Latin "a tongue understanded of the people"—to wit, the King's English? In short, for all the prayer book's undoubted beauty, life had moved on. Was it not time the church moved on also? Certainly other mainline churches had begun asking the same question, generally answering with a hearty nod of the head. The old language seemed, well, old. Even the Roman Catholic Church undertook about the same time to freshen up the Mass with modern language that quickly, and predictably, drove away the ancient Latin forms. As liturgy conformed itself to contemporary styles and tastes, even the beloved King James Version of the Bible fell into disuse. Yes—life had moved on.

One Anglican liturgical expert noted how, even in the nineteenth century, men had begun to recognize "the needs of a society whose characteristics were shaped by industry and technology, rather than by agriculture," a society in which "worship had to become more varied and more intense, rather than uniform, and leisurely." A modern and more complex society, in other words, was unlikely to content itself with the modes of a simpler, statelier time. A study of the prayer book, performed in the 1960s, complained of "long sentences, which, however beautiful in balance, modulation, and rhythm, make difficult a comprehension by modern congregations of its wondrous communication of the gospel." A future bishop involved in liturgical reform called prayer book style "rather talky and preachy." Still another study pointed to the growing prominence in life of visual images bidding fair to jostle aside mere words. Bishop Paul Moore, as he was wont to do, summed up pungently: "[W]e in the church . . . are stifled by seventeenth-century language and medieval thought forms."

Among those "thought forms" was acute consciousness of sin, a consciousness so acute, indeed, as potentially to drive away anyone who, like the Hepburn character, considered himself, on the whole, a pretty good Joe, needing relatively little (as the prayer book called it) "amendment of life." The Episcopal Church took sin with great seriousness, in accordance with the Anglican notion of God's supreme authority. The reformers had embedded in the consciousness of the Anglican worshipper the conviction of his own unworthiness before God—hence his dependence on the freely offered grace and mercy of Christ. There was something wrong with all of us, something *really* wrong. Ah, but it could be fixed. That was what really mattered. Christ had died on the cross for our sins, then ascended to heaven, where he waited to enfold in loving arms the sinner brought to repentance and amendment of life. What preceded repentance, of course, was the act of owning up.

Thus, in the service of Morning Prayer, worshippers would lament that "we have erred and strayed from thy ways like lost sheep" (a moment as lovely as it was theologically germane). At

Holy Communion, the obligation was to "acknowledge and bewail our manifold sins and wickedness, which we from time to time most grievously have committed, By thought, word, and deed, Against thy divine majesty, Provoking most justly thy wrath and indignation against us." It was not a particularly modern thing to say. And worse, from some standpoints, was to come. Another breath, and Anglicans found themselves declaring the "burden" of their sins to be "intolerable."

Now really. "Intolerable"? That meant something large and decisive had to be done about the matter, something likely to impinge unpleasantly on daily routine, as well as on self-esteem. Were matters as grim as all that? Much might be, indeed probably was, wrong with created humanity. Yet, as moderns believed themselves to have learned from Freud and other teachers, outside factors often left their mark: the cruelty of a father or mother; the depredations of the economic order; a careless word or two heard and taken to heart; even an accidental circumstance seen in retrospect as shaping future choices. Could we really help ourselves?

In any event, what about sin's public and corporate character, as expressed in social institutions like racial segregation? More and more the question would haunt us as the 1960s and 1970s wore on and critics of "the establishment"—from platforms inside and outside the churches—touted the duty of social action. Which was deadlier, political and social oppression, or the quest for good sex? If, in the church's view (as the church's detractors limned it), sin and sex were the same, that told us a thing or two about sin and its supposed importance in daily life.

This was because, in the 1960s, sex talk was beginning to regain the daily centrality it had enjoyed during the 1920s. It was back to flagellating (so to speak) the Victorians for having made sex seem dirty and disreputable, when in fact it was—ah, just *look*! And did we ever look: *Playboy*, topless actresses, soft-core porn, hard-core porn, hippie "love-ins," co-ed dorms, etc. Not that twentieth-century America had turned into Caligulan Rome. Human experience demonstrates that when it comes to sex, theory normally outruns practice. Still, the perception rapidly grew that yesterday's sexual norms might be losing their relevance. If "dirty old sex" was becoming okay, where did that leave other impeachments of human desire—the specifics within the generality called sin?

Increasingly the things that the prayer book said about sin and its awful consequences struck many moderns as exaggerated. As one architect of the liturgical changes then afoot commented, "[T]he language strikes many serious Christians of the late twentieth century as exaggerated. There never seems to be a chance to express the unfettered joy which Christ's death and resurrection accomplish." Not that the gentleman wanted to "minimize sin." He did want to emphasize hope, in a way that the present prayer book failed to do. What the prayer book lacked, as some thoughtful Episcopalians saw it, was a vocabulary of affirmation. The prayer book was rather sniffy toward mere men and women, always affirming their contingency and dependency rather than their raw potential. Where was the joy in all this, where the inspiration?

The fast-changing culture of the late twentieth century was much taken with the idea of progressivity—of forward movement, that is to say. Redemption came not only from the outside (the Cross) but also from within, as human beings mustered, organized, networked, picketed, marched, voted, volunteered, counseled, gave money, formed organizations and committees for this purpose and that one. None of which was, on its face, worrisome or despicable. The challenge for the church was to learn to distinguish secular reasonings and endeavors from theological ones, and then to exhibit the latter with more determination than the former. Not all Episcopalians cared for such an undertaking. Without minimizing sin, they wanted to avoid maximizing it, as many were coming to think the church had done for too long.

As if none of these rationales sufficed to justify reappraisal of the prayer book's content and structure, there were other motives. Major Christian communions were learning about the worship practices of the early Roman-era church. Certain scholars saw the prayer book as well enough for its time, the Reformation, but sadly detached on that account from knowledge and insights at the disposal of Christian neighbors.

A signal point concerned change itself. Who could argue plausibly that Christian practice had been frozen in time by divine command? Over thousands of dawns and days, suns had risen and set. New ways of understanding and doing had arisen. Christian practice had changed within to mention only one venerable and sacred outpost: Anglicanism. The prayer book itself represented Archbishop Cranmer's seemingly inspired overhaul of more ancient liturgies, such as the Catholic rites of Sarum and York, used widely in England at the time of the Reformation. The royal regime backing up Cranmer had gone so far as to forbid the use of Latin—never mind the imputed holiness of the old forms, or the devout associations they brought to mind. Everything from there on was to be in English. Practice would accommodate itself to circumstances. For the modern church, the question was not, change—yes or no? The question was, change—how deep, how thorough, how far-reaching?

Not since 1928 had the Episcopal Church revised the Book of Common Prayer. The reform of that day had been a gently modernizing one, virtually all the familiar language left intact; a few additions, a few subtractions; nothing to excite vocal dismay. Reform of that character—carried out while America danced and swigged its way through the Jazz Age—required a certain respectful, non-Jazz Age spirit, ready to confer on the established order the benefit of the doubt. If such a spirit had animated the Episcopal Church in the 1920s, by the 1960s it had taken flight, with bruises and gashes to show for the brief resistance it had put up. The 1960s were more than accidentally radical; they were determinedly radical. The why and the how of it could be hard to understand at the time; for that matter, they still baffle.

Beginning with the mid-1960s, change became a massive wave—a massive series of massive waves—crashing upon sunny beaches where the lazy expectation had been, up until then, more sun, and still more. In the 1960s, protective umbrellas collapsed, and the shifting sands redistributed familiar landmarks.

Hair grew long, then longer. Manners relaxed, then dissolved. A culture based on drug use appeared, put down roots, grew, seeded the landscape, took on quasi-religious status. Sex, for all its evident popularity, was a part of a larger whole. The old norms and notions, the one-time rules and prescriptions—whatever seemed to hem in and confine came under challenge. The whole notion of authority had fallen into disrepute.

Few of us milling around the Phoenix airport, or practically any other gathering place, prior to Christmas 1963, could have sensed, except in the vaguest way, the magnitude of the changes at hand. Yes, new hairstyles and musical styles might be on the way, but already we had accommodated Elvis Presley and Jerry Lee Lewis and ducktails and crewcuts. Life had somehow gone on, its largely even tenor not much disturbed. Suddenly, as it seemed, college students began defiantly puffing joints and demonstrating against a war conducted by their own country, if you could believe such a thing. A few genuinely hard-core types manufactured bombs or robbed banks. In radical circles, "the pigs" became a common term for the police. The United States itself

was widely excoriated as "Fascist-pig Amerika," the "k" an assertion of fancied links between the protestors' own country and
Herr Hitler's milieu.

New Left orators exhorted young people never to trust anyone
over thirty, a category including, of course, everyone from their
parents on up to the president and beyond. The same went for
the church, of course. And for the heads of great universities.
And for winners of the Nobel Prize. The bottom, I think, may
have been plumbed when newspapers noted the anger of Rickey
Ivie, a black teenager. This individual, wondrous to relate, had
discovered Johann Sebastian Bach to be nothing but an "old dead
punk." The papers deemed this dismissal worth our knowing. As
it was. It helped us grasp the degree to which anarchy appeared to
have become our cultural theme. Nobody, it sometimes appeared,
liked anybody any more.

Such was the environment in which prayer book revision
first captured the attention of the Episcopal Church. Abandoned
and zany the 1920s might have been, but not like this: angry,
resentful, contemptuous, both disoriented and disorienting. If
worship styles necessarily reflect the worshippers' times, it was
easy to know at the start of the revision process that the new
styles would unsettle.

They did. And do. The divide in the country, over Vietnam,
drugs, and so on, foreshadowed the divide opening in the Episcopal Church over prayer book revision: on one side (generally speaking), the church's ordained and elected leadership,
touting a dramatically "modernized" prayer book; on the other
side (generally speaking), lay men and women, and the clergy of
smaller parishes, urging respect for the old book and caution in
overhauling it. No defender of the old book called it strictly and
forever untouchable. A careful, narrowly tailored revision could
have won general acclaim. The revision put before the church

gradually, in stages, beginning in the late 1960s, was anything but careful. It struck many Episcopalians as a feat of learned pandering: the church permitting the standards and approach of the modern world to set the terms of worship.

Instead of a book of "common prayer"—the ideal of the English reformers, with all Anglicans expected to hear and speak the same words—the revisers of the old book, under supervision of the church's Standing Liturgical Commission, produced side-by-side texts. One was in "modern" English, the other in purportedly "traditional" language. That is, for the Eucharist (the old book's Holy Communion, inoffensively renamed), Morning and Evening Prayer, and Burial. Not for Baptism, nor for Confirmation, nor for Marriage—those services the revisers slyly saw as the province of the young, to whose comfort and understanding the church was attending.

The traditional language alternatives were a sop to supposed old fogies over whose dead bodies new ways and new language would have to be imposed. The traditional language service of burial spoke blatantly to this perception: If we can't turn 'em, the revisers seemed to be saying, we'll plant 'em—eventually. The Psalter, containing the one hundred and fifty psalms of David, was similarly translated into the tongue of the daily newspapers.

The church decided to move experimentally, labeling the new rites "proposed," testing them in regular Sunday worship. On ears appreciative of the old sublimities the new plain-talk fell harshly, and roused some to anger. The great majority of clergy and bishops, the professional class, appeared to accept the new regime with equanimity. By contrast, the pews smoked with resentment. The syndicated columnist James Jackson Kilpatrick, an Episcopalian, accused the revisionists of "liturgical butchery." A lay-led organization, the Society for the Preservation of the Book of Common Prayer, arose, its center of gravity in the ven-

erated English department of Vanderbilt University. The society's aim was to show ordinary Episcopalians what a crime their
church was contemplating and thus to block adoption of the new
book by the church's General Convention. The SPBCP published
well-grounded critiques of the new rites but failed to shake the
lassitude or, it might have been, the fatalism of fellow Episcopalians accustomed to taking, with gentility and a highball, their
directives from above. Episcopalians, sons and daughters of the
establishment, have over the years made generally substandard
rebels and warriors—unlike Southern Baptists, who in my experience love a good intra-church spat almost as much as they do an
altar call. At the 1973 General Convention the new prayer book
passed decisively its decisive test. The church meant to have a
new book. This was the book it meant to have.

Adoption was more easily voted than brought to effect. Whole
congregations, and groups within other congregations, bridled.
Their book was the old book. No church convention was going
to wrest it from them, especially, perhaps, at a historical moment
when so many certainties were disappearing. Thus the distrust
and acrimony—which reached a pitch previously unknown
in Episcopal history, except before and during the 1861–1865
unpleasantness—continued. Though, indeed, as church authorities had foreseen, the furor lessened as one funeral followed
another and survivors came to accept, even to relish, the new
order of things. The controversy over the prayer book, as I have
noted, is not much alluded to now, or even remembered with any
vividness, but, again as I have noted, it brought into focus issues
and concerns, not all of them evident at the time, that would
shape the church in succeeding years.

The liturgical butchers, by the time they downed their knives
and cleavers, had more than carved up a once-fetching, once-uni-
tive, liturgy. They had left the Episcopal Church with a new way

of speaking to its members, and to the world. As we all know, language is much more than grunts and acclamations, sounds and syllables. Sounds and syllables order thinking, as the revisers must have noted whenever they thought of the changes that came upon the Catholic church of England as Latin went out and English came in. All of a sudden, the laity became participants rather than dumb spectators. Turn a spectator into a participant and consequences of all sorts creep quietly into the church. A participant, for one thing, will have his own ideas as to what should be done, and how, and how quickly.

In like manner, the introduction of new forms and patterns into the church's worship was certain to increase the acceptance of modernity in guises other than the purely linguistic. If the Episcopal Church was going to accommodate, and even welcome, twentieth-century modes of speaking, the odds increased that twentieth-century modes of thinking would also settle themselves in the pew. The new prayer book no doubt helped fix the mind of the church more precisely on the world outside the church, the very outcome for which thinkers like Jim Pike and Paul Moore had been clamoring. It was easier now to address the world, using the tongue of the world. A sense of identity with the world and its concerns was bound to increase.

Was this so bad a thing? Not altogether. Much depended on how one defined the world's needs and concerns and measured them against the church's acknowledged duties, of which the foremost was presentation of the Gospel. On the one hand, the church might find it easier to present the Gospel in readily understood language, making due allowance for the disappearance of much reverence and beauty that went with the old language. On the other hand, undue identification with the wants of the world, rather than with its needs as Christianity defined them (repentance, forgiveness, salvation), posed potential dangers.

Most frightening of those dangers was the prospect of ministering to the world on the world's terms, not the church's. Into that precise trap walked the Episcopal Church—cheerily, cockily, with the new, nearly one-thousand-page, Book of Common Prayer in its hand. No foe of the new book was ready to say there was *no* good in it whatever. Certainly the service moved faster than before, with long, dense passages—especially those read by the clergy—having disappeared from the text and shorter acclamations having been introduced for the sake of what we might call audience participation. Anglo-Catholics rejoiced to find that the prayer book now embodied their contention that the central act of Christian worship was the Eucharist, not Morning Prayer or Evening Prayer, accompanied by Sermon. (A leader of the revision movement, writing not long before the Deluge, had urged making the Eucharist "a visible triumph in the Church's life of an order of justice, mercy, and love, of which the world cannot conceive.") Anglo-Catholic adherence to the book set it on a faster track to adoption than would have been the case otherwise.

Episcopalians of all varieties relished the variety they found in a book heavy on alternatives, at least of a certain sort. (Lovers of the old Psalter were out of luck: There was just the new, modern translation.) No longer were things to be the same way, always and everywhere. Modernity—automobile models galore, vitamins of every kind, a multiplicity of artificial sweeteners—had caught up with and surpassed medieval rigor. If society enjoyed opportunities of various sizes and descriptions, in all departments of life, why not the church as well? Where one rule, one mode, had worked in the past for the church, Episcopalians, it seemed increasingly clear, were entitled to spread their wings, to go places previously unexplored in order to see what was there, and how or whether it worked.

Amid the intoxicating variety, there was, nevertheless, a sizable problem. It was what the church had decided to do about the sin problem—namely, to give the matter a more modern spin. It might be true that Christians came in all sizes and colors. Was there, nevertheless, no common denominator? As it happened, there was. Sin was its name. It came in the box, with the human condition. Indeed, it *was* the human condition. Nor was sex the whole of it.

"In Adam's fall/we sinned all," the embroidered samplers from colonial times had said. No reputable theologian had ever argued otherwise. Sin, by any name, was separation from God. It involved, as with Eve, in *Genesis*, the exaltation of the will over that obedience and humility owed the Creator of all things. Much mention of sin, as noted above, might sadden or even depress worshippers intent on joy. Well, it was supposed to, you know.

Now regular, written confessions of wrongdoing can become routine, or they can be read through—the really abasing parts, that is—with crossed fingers and mental reservations. An "intolerable" burden? Of the powerful and the educated, who out of proportion to their American numbers attended Episcopal worship that could be asking a great deal. And yet, theologically, there could be no shirking the exercise. We just plain weren't as good as we might think. Though some, ah, softenings, some throttling downs, might not come amiss.

The liturgical butchers had not fallen to work with a public commitment to degrade the place of sin in Episcopal affairs. No self-respecting Christian church was going to throw out the door the understanding of sin as the dissonant factor in man's relationship to God, but there are ways of talking about sin, and then there are ways. Was it necessary to confess flatly the lack of "health" in us? Not as the revisers saw things. Out, from the Morning Prayer service, went that particular formula for abasement. More telling, because of the church's claim to have recovered Eucharistic centrality, was what happened with the Eucharistic service.

The revisers sought to lower, insofar as they could, the confessional temperature. In "Rite I," a pacifier for Episcopalians who loved the old language and might consider themselves at least occasionally "wicked," the traditional confession was left standing, though an alternative form was inserted. It was a cheap enough concession to those nearer the Pearly Gates, chronologically speaking, than the audience at which the revisers aimed—the coming generation; the young, the flexible, the supposedly un-ossified. For these there was "Rite II" and modern language of the sort their culture already embraced. What were these to say against themselves and their deportment? "We confess that we have sinned against you [God, that is], in thought, word, and deed, by what we have done, and by what we have left undone. We have not loved you with our whole heart; we have not loved our neighbors as ourselves. We are truly sorry, and we humbly repent."

No flushed faces, no dabbed handkerchiefs on perspiring brows in this theological climate! The once-wicked are "sorry" for any difficulties their conduct, their contemplations, might have caused the Lord. Not grieved, not anguished—sorry. In "sorriness," the terribleness of offering offense to God recedes from view.

It would be nice if the whole problem were linguistic. Twenty-first-century dictionaries contain the right words for expressing wretchedness over repeated offenses against God. The *desire* to find such words and measure them out—that might be the difficulty. The old prayer book of the Episcopal Church took for granted the asymmetries of the relationship between man and God and the former's capacity for playing hob and raising hell. The new book presumed a God both more relaxed and accessible than the avatars that terrified medieval peasants and intimidated Tudor and Stuart worthies. We had not previously known this God, or known Him well, anyway. Here he was, no more the celestial autocrat staring down from his throne (which might or might not be a real seat) in heaven (which might or might not be a real place) and judging (a little callously, it sometimes seemed) all the tiny beings below. The God of the new prayer book seemed a particularly nice God, not without standards but willing to accept variant viewpoints, little disposed to insist on Just One Right Way. You could call such a God modern—very modern.

That was because "the sins of the world," in the phraseology of the old prayer book, were taking on, as the world saw it, a different cast. Sins had been spiritual and moral before. Now they were social and political. They were not sins at all, in the proper sense, as pertaining to the human condition *vis-à-vis* God. For such offenses the 1960s and 1970s cared less and less. What these feverish decades did oppose or profoundly suspect was racism, sexism, militarism, air pollution, corporate extortion, and the like. Such concerns might have some theological character, but, more to the immediate point, all were hugely, immensely, overwhelmingly secular. There was a common denominator. All were sins against the Outcast, or the Downtrodden, whoever he might be, wherever he might live. And the sinner—who was he? The world could answer such a question easily: America, the nation, was the sinner. Particular Americans, by virtue not of their human flesh but of their citizenship in this oppressive nation, had consciously or unconsciously supported their country's terrible aims.

Vietnam, as anti-warriors, on campus and off, regularly told the story, was an American war against brown people halfway around the world, an interruption of their quest for self-determination, even that form of self-determination the Viet Cong were determined to enforce by bullet and bomb. The proclamation of

America's social sins hardly stopped at the Gulf of Tonkin and the South China Sea. It appeared, suddenly, that America, which had fought a bloody war to free its own slaves, was the premier oppressor of black people and also of Indians (known more and more frequently as Native Americans). Likewise, America oppressed women of all colors, including white, chaining them to kitchen sinks and denying them opportunity in the broadest sense. Yes, America likewise oppressed those Americans who sought sexual fulfillment in ways of their own choosing, rather than in the tiresome ways so long enforced by the narrowly religious. As a people, it seemed, we were awful, excepting, naturally, those who took it on themselves to assure us of our awfulness, and then to remedy it.

The Episcopal Church's turn from judgment, in the framing of its new prayer book, seems no coincidence whatsoever. Against the backdrop of cultural struggle, what was the likelihood, really, of a new prayer book's ratifying the steady, consistent viewpoints of bygone centuries? The new prayer book was, among many other things, a gesture of weariness with a world that regarded personal guilt as of extraordinary importance. Surely by now we had moved beyond the merely personal. Guilt now was collective. Not that that freed the Episcopal Church, in its own narrowed eyes, from the obligation of addressing that guilt, rebuking it, rectifying it.

SIX ≈
Womanpower

O
N JUST ONE THEORETICAL POINT PRACTICALLY EVERYONE, I think, will concur. It is that nothing happens overnight, appearing on the human doorstep dripping with dew and begging for, or demanding, a seat at the breakfast table. Nothing "just happens." There are seeds and roots, ancestors and forerunners.

If, to put matters another way, sex was ever, anywhere, for a single moment, out of sight as a popular concern and obsession, all I can say is, no one noticed. Which is why I would claim it was never at any time out of sight. Sex *is* human life, the means of projecting humanity into the future, all the while providing modes and models of human connection.

The historic Christian conviction, rooted in Scripture, is of sex as a means not to mankind's own ends but rather to God's. "It is he that hath made us, and not we ourselves," reads Psalm 100, as Episcopalians once regularly recited it in Morning Prayer. "[W]e are his people, and the sheep of his pasture." All this, naturally, followed from the pivotal account in Genesis, as the King James Version expressed the matter: "And God created man in his own image; in the image of God created he him."

The sponginess of a word like "created" should keep no one from acknowledging that to be Christian, or, indeed, Jewish, is to live in the bonds of responsibility and accountability to God the Father Almighty, Maker of heaven and earth, as the Creed of the Apostles makes him known. Anglican liturgy was—is—full of affirmation of God's unchallengeable sovereignty. There is, for instance, the *Te Deum Laudamus,* an ancient acclamation of the church: "We praise thee, O God, we acknowledge thee to be the Lord. All the earth doth worship thee: the Father everlasting."

What did God want, then, and where did sex fit in? The Episcopal Church, whose ideas on the subject were essentially the same as those of other Christian bodies, spoke to that question in the marriage rite. Holy Matrimony signified "the mystical union that is betwixt Christ and his Church." This made it of large account. The English prayer book of 1662 specified matrimony's chief purposes: "the procreation of children," "a remedy against sin, and to avoid fornication," and "mutual society, help, and comfort" for the happy couple, but the Americans eliminated this accounting, cutting to the practicalities. The couple would love, comfort, honor, and keep each other, with equal diligence on each side. Then they would "so live together in this life, that in the world to come [they might] have life everlasting."

This was no mere human merger; it was a relationship with God himself, in keeping with God's own specifications. What, no latitude for expression? Some latitude, certainly—just not as much as the culture was beginning to claim for itself as the twentieth century unfolded.

Not that a few usually muttered words could possibly convey the wisdom of the Christian faith, or for that matter of humanity in general, concerning the meaning of marriage. It is important to note that no one individual, not even a singularly inspired convention of theologians, worked out that meaning, then set it among us for admiration. By experience and divine prompting, mankind had come to see marriage-with-sex and sex-with-marriage, not as *a* way of living and experiencing, but rather as *the* way. As Roger Scruton duly notes, "In all observed societies some form of marriage exists, as the means whereby the work of one generation is dedicated to the well-being of the next. Marriage does not merely protect and nurture children; it is a shield against sexual jealousy and a unique form of social and economic cooperation, with a mutually supported division of roles that more than doubles the effectiveness of each partner in their shared bid for security." Accordingly it enjoys "a distinct social aura." With so much going for it, you might suppose marriage to be the very instrument of God for the building up of His kingdom. As it happens, Christians made, and make, just that supposition.

But then things got murky, as things generally do amid such a clamor of voices as commenced in the 1960s. The culture, in the twentieth century's closing decades, undertook to redefine sex and sexual relationships in ways that gave short shrift to the old norms. While the culture talked, the Episcopal Church, a designated custodian of the old norms, listened intently. It nodded. It smiled understandingly. By the end of the century, the old norms concerning sexual interactivity were no more, and most of Christianity was bending over backwards to affirm and advance the new order of things. Women were functioning as Episcopal priests and bishops. One of these, as I have noted—the aforementioned Mrs. Jefferts Schori—became presiding bishop of the Episcopal Church in November 2006. Similarly, in 2006, deputies of the Church, at General Convention, elected a woman as their presiding officer.

A substantial number of faithful Episcopalians—women and lovers of women—looked upon the new dispensation with shock and wonder. They asked, with some anxiety, was the new dispensation calibrated to cultural promptings, or to authentic Christian understandings? It was not easy to be sure.

If the Episcopal Church reflected to whatever degree the culture of which it was a constituent element, it was going to note, at a minimum, the culture's attitudes. How it was going to witness to those attitudes was another matter. Would it challenge, and try to reshape, such attitudes as seemed contrary to Christian witness and belief, or would it find those attitudes congenial, perhaps inspirational? A few necessary words, first, concerning the attitudes in question, and their point of origin. In the mid-1960s it was as plain as day that a revolution was sweeping much of the country, not to mention Western Europe. Nor had the revolution pounced at that instant from some dark closet. It had been coming on for some time. Its roots, especially its American roots, were struck deep in the American way of affirming and reaffirming the doctrine of human equality. Were not all men "equal" (the term "men" doing double duty for the two sexes)? There was not much getting around Mr. Jefferson's intention of linguistically erasing most, if not all, basic human distinctions.

Ever since, the nation had worked sporadically, and with varying degrees of enthusiasm, at the task of formally leveling those distinctions. Property qualifications for voting fell by the wayside early in the nineteenth century. A bit later, the slaves were freed, though for various and complicated reasons the nation decided that freedom, as opposed to full equality, for the former slaves would suffice, at least for a while. Women of all races remained officially subordinate to men: politically, inasmuch as they were barred from voting, and even theologically, with Christianity affirming or at least implying strongly the authority of men, husbands in particular. Not that such a state of affairs erased from many men's minds the deep suspicion that, from behind their lace-trimmed fans, women actually ran the joint. Growing numbers of women, nevertheless, sought constitutional as well as social confirmation of their worth. A few began to clamor for what we nowadays would call "empowerment." They demanded, for starters, the vote. Underlying that demand was the hope, the wish, the ambition to be seen as no less worthy of general respect, and of opportunity, than their hubands.

There was nothing peculiarly American about the clamor that men began to notice as emanating from wives and sisters and, now and then, mothers. Wars and revolutions in Europe, from the eighteenth century forward, had unsettled complacent ways of thinking about human relationships. Once you uncrown a king, or come near it, you expose all manner of possibilities for the narrowing or closing of social gaps. By 1861, John Stuart Mill was ready to argue, in his essay "The Subjection of Women," that "the principle which regulates the existing social relations between the two sexes—the legal subordination of one sex to the other—is wrong in itself, and now one of the chief hindrances to human improvement; and that it ought to be replaced by a principle of perfect equality."

American women acquired the vote—that this was a gift from their men-folk is a point too little acknowledged—immediately following World War I. Events of even more profound significance were soon to follow. There occurred, almost overnight, what Frederick Lewis Allen, the period's wisest social chronicler, called "a revolution in manners and morals." "It was the girls," said Allen, "who started it. Did mothers think of corsets as the armor of respectability? A great many daughters decided that dancing without a corset was much more personal and satisfactory. Did mothers think young girls shouldn't drink? Daughters found that a gulp of illegal whiskey from the hip flask of a swain

97

in a parked sedan added an excellent note of zest to the proceedings. Did mothers converse in ladylike circumlocutions? Daughters talked right out about sex and the libido, the latter being a word one got from Freud, who had said, according to report, that "repressions were bad for you."

And so on: the whole country, seemingly, loosening its buttons, hanging up its Victorian inhibitions on the garden trellis. Cole Porter, in the early 1930s, would slyly epitomize the matter: "Anything goes." (And he hadn't even seen the 1960s!) The Depression understandably calmed things down for a time. But in 1941 came America's entry into World War II, whose unprecedented manpower demands caused factories to fill with women, and whose tumult and grim desperation relaxed further the moral norms loosened by the previous world war. Once the postwar marriage and baby booms ran their course, it should have puzzled no one that womanhood was ready to set off again on its quest.

The first swallow of the new springtime, so to speak, was a vaguely discontented housewife named Betty Friedan, who gave tongue in 1963 to the discontents women supposedly were experiencing. She named the problem "the problem that has no name." Which meant? On Friedan's showing, it meant acknowledgment by women of "a strange stirring, a sense of dissatisfaction, a yearning." Which yearning was for? No one could answer such a question precisely. One could back into it, nonetheless: What women had in the way of material comforts and patriarchal protection fell short somehow of what was essential.

"American women are kept from growing to their full human capacities," Friedan declared. The dire consequences included emotional breakdown, alcoholism, and suicide. "If we continue to produce millions of young mothers who stop their growth and education short of identity, without a strong core of human values to pass on to their children, we are committing, quite simply, genocide."

Friedan titled her book *The Feminine Mystique*. It became the founding document of the new feminism, awakened—and by no Prince Charming—from its long prewar and postwar slumber. If not all American women by any means felt the twinges of discontent that Betty Friedan had described, still those who did feel them put remarkable energy, and sometimes equally remarkable anger, into the search for the cure.

The voices of women helped swell the chorus of liberation begun by blacks (most of them men, as it happened, except for Rosa Parks, Fannie Lou Hamer, and a few others). A "women's liberation" movement took flesh, demanding changes in the relationship between men and women—a relationship forged over the centuries by law, literature, custom, music, and, often enough, it seemed, by sheer male dominance and lack of consideration. The bill of particulars lengthened almost every day. "Male chauvinism" inhibited women's quest for wider opportunities in the world! And fed violence against women! Why couldn't men help more around the house, and why was a woman's right to sexual expression less important than a man's? Language itself was a barrier to true equality: "chair*man*," "fire*man*," even "*man*-kind"! Brassieres were a symbol of male dominance! What was "chivalry" but patronization and putdown? In public discourse, "sexist" became the standard argument-ending rebuke to male pretensions, a term on a rhetorical par with "racist" or "fascist."

Clearly something like root-and-branch revolution was brewing. Forget the placid, consensual spirit of the 1950s. In the 1960s, things were going to be different, not to mention juster, kinder, and more egalitarian. Nor just in the matter of custom. Law, a great shaper of custom, had to change as well. What was wanted were constitutional amendments, both at the state and the federal level, establishing forever the principle of equality between men and women. From 1973 forward a decision of the U.S. Supreme Court would symbolize the new order. Abortion, said the court's 7–2 majority, was a constitutionally protected choice.

Roe v. *Wade*, by proclaiming a general indifference as to the termination of unborn life, did overthrow the accrued moral wisdom of Christianity, as well as the secular viewpoint that government had the duty of protecting life. And yet, as law, the *Roe* decision merely amplified the growing conviction that choice was the touchstone of modern human affairs. Not to choose wisely but just to *choose* was becoming the wisdom of the day, a block to long-held teachings about "right" and "wrong." Could it be that these familiar terms merely described individual perceptions and tastes? Did there really exist some abstract, overarching Right over against some equally overarching Wrong? If not, a great many moral teachers were going to be out of jobs, unless they adapted themselves, and their views, to the new order.

It would be unkind to suggest that Episcopal theologians and bishops and pastors struck their moral colors and ran up the skull and crossbones of "liberation" just to keep their jobs and credibility. Motives aside, it would be neither unkind nor unfair to say the Episcopal Church abandoned with precipitate haste its understanding of the male-female relationship. Of the principal Christian folds, Episcopalians seem, at least since the 1970s, the most ardently feminist.

"Why?" and "How?" are the questions before the house.

Note that "the murky realm of motive," as Theodore Roosevelt called it, is a generally unsafe place to venture. We find, if we do go there, a terrain marked by jagged rocks and quicksands, each with its own warning signs or temptations. It is better on the whole not to attempt a description of what lies hidden in another's mind. How, then, to talk about the Episcopal Church and its present policies toward women? Perhaps by remarking, first, on the church's culture—indeed, the culture of almost any church.

To say that Christian churches depend extraordinarily on women is to say only the obvious. Look around an ordinary service in an ordinary church on an ordinary Sunday. What do we see—serried ranks of males? Likelier we see pews packed, to the extent that pews anywhere these days are packed, chiefly with women, not a few seeming rooted to the place, with their gray buns and long memories of dead rectors, rubber-tipped canes guiding them to the altar, arthritic hands cupped humbly at chin level at the approach of the Body of Christ.

"Without women," according to a Barna Research Group study as the twentieth century wound up, "Christianity would have nearly 60 percent few adherents. . . . Christianity is still the 'faith-of-choice' among Americans, but particularly among women," 90 percent of whom identified themselves as Christian, compared to 83 percent of men. Not a huge gap there, and yet a gap of some consequence.

Why such a gap in the first place, though? Maledom and religion hardly contradict each other. The Savior was male; likewise his apostles; likewise, self-evidently, the "Fathers of the Church"; likewise bishops, popes, cardinals, and varied communicators of the Gospel. St. Paul had strongly advised, in the first letter to the Corinthians, against letting women's voices be heard in the church. It was a viewpoint that certainly informed Dr. Johnson's famous response to Boswell's account of a woman's preaching to a Quaker meeting. The feat, said Johnson, was like "a dog's walking on his hinder legs; it is not done well, but you are surprised to find it done at all."

Keep an eye steadily on prelates and preachers, nevertheless, and you miss much. You miss the angels of mercy, the dispensers of prayer and comfort, and of spiritual steadiness and encouragement in the midst of ruin and temptation. You miss, in fine, the multitude of Episcopal (and Methodist and Catholic and Baptist, etc.) women without whose labors and prayers no church could have lasted. It was not that women made no (what to say—historic?) contributions to the church. It was not that at all. There were women martyrs and women missionaries; there were women who organized and dispensed Christian comfort, and other women who wrote wisely of spiritual matters. Furthermore, the Savior who became man had done so through the immediate agency of a mother, known in Catholic jurisdictions as *Regina Coeli,* the Queen of Heaven.

With it all, women appeared to have a special vocation, that of seeing the church through the just plain dailiness of life and activity, involving themselves in its work, making certain the job gets done. A trio of sociologists in the late 1960s, saying nothing that daily experience had not fortified already, pronounced the church "a more salient institution for women than for men." As for Episcopal women, said the three (Charles Glock, Benjamin Ringer, and Earl Babbie), they were likelier than the menfolk to attend church on Sundays and to become deeply involved in the church's organizational life. "Correspondingly, the church and religion are more salient for Episcopal women intellectually." Data suggested further that "lower status women turn to the Episcopal Church as a means of achieving the status they do not enjoy in the secular society."

I venture that an additional factor shaped Episcopal attitudes toward women—class. A church of the middle-to-upper classes enfolded many men of consciously progressive and enlightened views, unwilling or unable to quash their wives' and daughters' aspirations. Clarence Day, Sr., had been a patriarch of the Victorian school, a generous, if slightly blustery, *gentleman.* His like was rarely to be seen in the Episcopal Church of the 1960s and 1970s. Women and men now met at eye level.

The conjunction of culture and theology in the 1960s was nowhere more evident than in the arguments that sprang up in Christianity concerning the ordination of women as priests. While the culture was busily "empowering" women in general, on the assumption their lot had for too many years been one of rank subservience to the menfolk, particular women were beginning to clamor for admission to the Christian priesthood, for the right, that is, to take their places alongside men—if not majestically alone—at the altar, peforming the ancient sacraments of the Church. There were at the time few women ministers of any brand; there were no women priests at all. The Roman Catholic Church, the Eastern Orthodox church, and the worldwide Anglican Communion all reserved the priesthood for males.

A few words about the distinction between the two godly vocations, minister and priest: The Reformers of the sixteenth century had turned their backs on the concept of a priesthood that seemed (to the Reformers, though hardly to the priests) more jealous of perquisites and power than zealous for the Word of God. Where, asked the Reformers, did the priest get his dignity? Surely not from the Bible, which implied a general equality among Christ's followers. A faithful Christian man—it was always in those days a man—could read and understand the Bible once it had been translated into the vernacular, translation being a primary mission of the Reformers. Why could not this same authentically Christian man proclaim, through God's inspiration, the message of salvation through Christ? It was oral proclamation for which the reformers cared—the word, based on Holy Scripture and flung from the pulpit into the midst of sinners as a reproach or a comfort, but always as a call to repentance.

The mysteries of the altar were another matter: the priest, at the east end of the church, mumbling to himself the words by which, mysteriously, mere bread and wine became Christ's Body and Blood; a sometimes bored or distracted congregation not just physically but emotionally distant from the proceedings, watching rather than worshipping. If the Reformers, especially the Anglican Reformers, forbore from outright repudiation of the Mass as Sacrament, ordained by Christ himself "in the same night that he was betrayed," they toned down the mystery and the outcomes, threw some light and logic on the entire show.

From the regular and essential Christian action, the Mass, renamed by Anglicans the Lord's Supper, or Holy Communion (the title, the Eucharist, came much later to Anglicanism) became the exceptional occasion. Out went the muttered Latin which had inspired the popular phrase "hocus-pocus"; in came the solid cadences of English prose. The sermon, the unfolding of God's word before eyes blinded and hearts hardened, was now for English Christians the great event of Sunday. Not least because the theology of the communion was no longer as before. The Reformers saw to that. No more the transformation of wine and bread into Christ's own body and blood, in partial consequence of the priest's words and actions. The twenty-eighth of the Thirty-Nine Articles of Religion drawn up by the English Church in 1562 declared the former sacramental understanding "repugnant to the plain words of Scripture," as well as an inciter of superstition. In fact, Christ's Body was "given, taken, and eaten, in the Supper, only after an heavenly and spiritual manner."

So much for the custodians of the old mysteries—the priests. Or, anyway, so much for the old, unreformed character of their office, which now was to resume the shape of New Testament ministry, a shape (according to the Reformers) that medieval corruption had debased.

Among Anglicans, few of whom had wished to veer as far from Catholicism as did the Calvinists and Lutherans, the term "priest" never faded entirely from view. Archbishop Cranmer declined to strike it from the Book of Common Prayer. He provided, moreover, for the bishop to say, in laying hands on the head of a candidate for ordination, "Receive the Holy Ghost for the office and work of a Priest in the Church of God."

Over time, particular Anglicans would labor in particular ways for a higher sense of priestly function and vocation—less high than had been the pre-Reformation rule, yet higher than any sense the Reformers had entertained. Whereas in the novels of Jane Austen and Anthony Trollope the Anglican clergyman goes by plain old Mr. Thus-and-So, by the late nineteenth century, many clergy, both in Great Britain and in the United States, were claiming for themselves the title "Father," signifying a vocation set apart from other vocations by the act of ordination.

It was to this vocation that American women began ardently to aspire, once feminism had started smothering or shouting down familiar assumptions about the "proper" role of women. If late twentieth century women could be politicians, bankers, lawyers, and editors (not to mention plumbers, college presidents, bus drivers, and police officers), instead of merely teachers, secretaries, and tenders of the home fires, what, please, was the special problem with the Christian priesthood? Was there indeed such a problem, or was it just a case of longtime male tenants burrowed deep inside a male preserve, a kind of gentlemen's club they had no inclination to share with the Weaker Sex?

Late-twentieth-century feminism was dismissive of arguments having to do with the "natural" fitness of males for this secular prerogative or that one. It liked arguments for the all-male priesthood no better than it liked arguments for the supposed imprisonment of women in low-paying, unchallenging lines of work. Once the clamor to ordain women had begun, it was easy to predict in which direction things were headed.

Like their Roman Catholic and Orthodox brethren, Anglicans held, if sometimes a little mechanically, that men alone could occupy the sacred priesthood. A sense of patriarchal gentility might—*might!*—have reinforced the conviction, but the conviction itself had theological anchorage.

There were several aspects to the matter (of which I will say more in the next chapter), no one of them decisive for every purpose and in every dispute. Collectively, nonetheless, the arguments for male priesthood seemed massive, a mighty fortress guarding the innocence and devotion of the Church.

The weakness of the various arguments, if it is fair to call it weakness, lay in their inferential quality. That is, neither Matthew, nor Mark, nor Luke, nor John, had reported Christ as saying, "Naught but men shall minister at mine altar. And verily I *mean* it!" Even then, industrious lawyers could have fallen to work undermining the text. (Did "naught," in first-century parlance, mean what it means now?) And yet, as we know, unambiguous declarations of intent are hard to subvert, even in court.

The church had no such declarations on which to rely, but it had much else. To start, there was the historical record. Had Jesus called women to apostleship? Not if the Gospel accounts were to be seen as authentic (and if they were not, how much else in them had to be offloaded in modern times?). The Lord had called male disciples only, no matter his reverence for his mother or the generosity and consideration he showed female followers. As the present Roman Catholic catechism sums up the matter: "The Church recognizes herself to be bound by this choice made by the Lord himself." Then there was the evidence from St. Paul and other sources that the early church—the church closest in time and place to the Savior—had found for women genuinely important but always non-priestly roles. A complementary line of reasoning held that the priest, before he could stand in Christ's place at the altar, had in earthly respects fully to resemble Christ, who was after all the Son, not the Daughter, of God, and certainly not the sexless offspring.

All such considerations carried weight, not least on account of their durability. True, there was no clinching declaration from the Lord's own mouth that men alone were to function as priests. And yet, clearly, precedent and authority were on the side of those who argued for the all-male priesthood. That was precisely the trouble. Precedent and authority resonated weakly in the late twentieth century, more weakly, perhaps, than ever before, with those to whom the direction of human affairs had passed.

The more so because precedent and authority reinforced "patriarchalism." The whole notion of patriarchalism—society run by men, on behalf of men and women—was coming into disrepute by the 1970s. Never mind how the males of the Old and New Testaments had behaved, including that old misogynist St. Paul, with his injunctions about the duty of wives to "obey" their husbands. That had been another time and place. That Holy Scripture recorded and seemed to commend the standard male-female roles of ancient Palestine was one more proof that the Spirit had to be consulted in these matters in order to show us the new way of looking at things. Whatever modern America might be, it was emphatically not the Kingdom of Israel.

The problem was in some sense an *American* problem. That is, Americans had long been famous for their eagerness to dig up the established and plant things no one had planted before, to try out things and combinations not thitherto tried and to put them to the ultimate test, which was, simply: Did they work? Not that Americans had some constitutional aversion to tradition; they simply made less room for it in their national arrangements than did less dynamic peoples. America was nothing if not dynamic. And yet, even taking that national predisposition into account, the 1960s and 1970s proved a time of extraordinary willingness to throw over the side practically anything familiar from long use, except perhaps the bullhorns through which the prophets of the streets bawled their calls to rebellion and the pulp paper on which they cranked out denunciations of ideas no one before had dreamed of denouncing.

A point of equal heft is that the rebellion began as a war against perceived "privilege," specifically the privilege that a system of racial segregation had granted white Americans at the expense of black Americans. It was American women—anyway, those who claimed to speak for American women—who opened the second stage of the rebellion. They, too, wanted their rights, meaning their theological as well as occupational rights. Indeed, to many of the Episcopal women who sought admission to the priesthood, those rights were to be understood as identical. By denying them ordination, the church was suppressing their human rights.

It mattered little that the church's scruples in this matter were theologically grounded. To the extent that it did matter, supporters of women's ordination, including growing numbers of men, argued that the church had the theology wrong. Whatever reading of the situation might have made sense in the past made sense no longer. Times indeed had changed. The Holy Spirit had shown new ways of looking at old questions. Yes, and it was time we looked!

SEVEN

Pleased as Man with Us to Dwell

B Y NOW, MANY AMERICANS HAVE GROWN USED TO WOMEN priests and ministers. The Episcopalians have them—and women bishops as well. The Methodists have women clergy, as do the Presbyterians, the Lutherans, and so on. Truth be told, we have grown used to women everythings, including, due to the Iraq conflict, casualties of war. All of which feeds the common perception that there is nothing women can't do, given half a chance.

I note this in order to acknowledge how many reading these words are likely to shrug and say, "Women priests—so?" The "so" requires a different way of looking at the idea of the woman priest, and the Episcopal Church's part in making her a recognizable figure in modern culture. The "so" obliges us to do something distinctly un-contemporary, if not un-American—that is, to differentiate, to suggest that some things are not the same as others and that the blurring of identities, in modern egalitarian fashion, undermines the quest for truth and understanding. This way is no longer the Episcopal way, which I think it accurate to say is an immense part of the Episcopal problem.

A woman is not a man. A man is not a woman. We start there, before provoking a repeated query: "So?" A lot of what is today called "sexism" may well be embedded in persistent understandings of the differences between men and women. "Sexism," whatever such an emotionally loaded term might mean, would certainly be accounted symptomatic of mankind's fallen state, a consequence of original sin. Yet "sexism" and the intellectual acknowledgement of male-female distinctions are different commodities. Real life shows us this.

An example: For all that thousands of women now serve in the armed forces, public policy, as set by the U.S. government—a deliberately non-sexist enterprise—bars treatment of men and women as interchangeable units, like gallon cartons of milk. Two factors distinguish female soldiers from male soldiers. One is physical capability, related to height, bone structure, and so on. The other has to do with cultural, as well as theological, considerations. Women alone bear children; women, if nowadays in closer partnership with men, nurture children in a manner the most nurturing male is hard put to imitate. (Nor do I, as a father and grandfather, have the slightest hesitancy in making this claim.) It gets down to this: Women are worth shielding. They ensure the future. We acknowledge this with some unease, recognizing that to put men in the forefront of battle and women at the rear is to admit a distinction in human roles, an instance of radical inequality.

Does this "inequality," which is really more a matter of asymmetry than anything else, carry over into ecclesiastical matters? Let us just say Christians always assumed so. Can all the great Christians of yore have been hard-core misogynists? It hardly seems likely. What of Jesus himself, who called only male apostles, despite the latitude one might associate with divine sonship? Had he something against women? To say so would be to stand the scriptural record on its head. Our Lord drew women into profound communion with him: Mary and Martha, Mary Magdalene, the woman at the well, the woman taken in adultery, the woman who washed his feet with precious ointment, then dried them with her hair. (The hunger to believe in Jesus as husband of Mary Magdalene, central to the popularity of *The Da Vinci Code*, shows the importance to many women of seeing the Savior as a man like any other—except, presumably, neater in his personal habits.)

Above all women in Jesus' ambit stood, of course, his own mother, the Blessed Virgin, for whom, as St. John records, he took precious thought as he hung on the Cross. And no apostle argued then or afterwards for the radical inclusion of women into the priesthood? Why not? Because of cultural sexism? That would have been odd. Christianity defiantly confronted the world's most egregious human dysfunctions—pride, greed, lust, and the like—and bade its hearers throw off these spiritual encumbrances. Are we to assume the church of the martyrs, female and male alike, dithered, wobbled, scrambled away, in the presence of entrenched sexism? I wonder whether those who say so can have thought the matter through. Could they be projecting twenty-first-century egalitarian attitudes onto the picture screen of the first century A.D.? It seems to me we might at the very least entertain such a possibility.

We have grown used to women priests, yes. But it is not quite enough to say, that's that. We have grown used to this decided innovation just in the last couple of decades, which, *sub specie aeternitatis*, isn't much time at all, hardly enough time to appropriate online trading and compact fluorescent light bulbs into normal existence, or even to decide how large a car it makes sense nowadays to drive. Nor does the installation of a female presiding bishop for the Episcopal Church look like dispositive proof. Proof? What is "proof," anyway? None of us who write of these matters can "prove" we are right, beyond, as the fine old phrase has it, cavil or peradventure of a doubt.

What it is possible to do concerning the Episcopal Church's abandonment of the all-male priesthood is to look at how the decision has played out in real time. Is today's Episcopal Church a stronger, better, brighter witness to the truths of Christianity on account of admitting women to the priesthood? Or is the matter, let us just say, otherwise? And is one entitled to conclude that the heavy hand of modern culture covers and smothers the whole discussion, hard as we might try to fling it from us?

At its 1976 General Convention, held in Minneapolis, the Episcopal Church voted to make women eligible for ordination to the sacred order of priesthood. The decision involved a simple change in the canons, or internal laws, of the church. Yet the changes that ensued were in every sense extraordinary, likely the most momentous in all of Anglicanism's American history up to that point, throwing light or shadow (as you will) across the coming years.

Here was something startlingly new. Not just refreshed or refurbished, but new altogether in the history of those Christian communions, like Roman Catholicism, Orthodoxy, Anglicanism, committed officially to the witness of the early centuries.

True, Canadian Anglicans were at the time just weeks away from ordaining their first woman priest. Moreover, three American bishops, turning the civil disobedience styles of the 1960s to theological account, had already, as it were, crossed the line, ordaining eleven women deacons as priests in 1974—asking no permission to do so, and ready for the rebuke they received when a meeting of all Episcopal bishops declared the ordinations invalid. Here, all the same, in the autumn of 1976, was the Anglican franchise in the world's richest nation, in effect declaring the rebels right, while suggesting that the defenders of tradition were . . . you know, well-meaning people, possibly, but sadly behind the times, treading theological backwaters in which they might drown unless rescued against their apparent will.

It had generally been the way of the Episcopal Church to measure its thoughts and actions against the consensus of the faith, the timeless and unchanging faith, bearing the trademark of the apostles, who had been with the Lord, who had followed him, heard him, touched him, sobbed at Calvary, rejoiced at the empty tomb, and seen him taken up to heaven on a cloud. What they had known with certainty trumped what others might merely have guessed or supposed. Thus John: "This is the disciple who is bearing witness to these things, and who has written these things; and we know that his testimony is true."

As for the import of "these things," St. Paul, or, if one prefers, the anonymous author of the canonical epistles to Timothy, had enjoined the disciple Timothy to "Follow the pattern of the sound words which you have heard from me, in the faith and love which are in Christ Jesus" and to "guard the truth that has been entrusted to you by the Holy Spirit who dwells within us." There was much else of similar import from Paul, as from the multifarious teachers who followed him, century after century, millennium after millennium, relating what the late-nineteenth-century American hymn would name, with affection, "the old, old story/ Of Jesus and his love."

Light and truth had come into the world in Jesus Christ. The Christian teacher was no fabulist, no tavern teller of war stories; he was a faithful witness, passing on without embroidery the testimony of other faithful witnesses. A witness reading into sights and events whatever his fancy suggested was no witness at all.

He was a fraud. On his jagged deceptions innocent souls might come to shipwreck, lured to the rocks by what was not, and never could be, the truth.

Here was the question when it came to ordaining women as priests. Did the idea match up with reality—the reality of God? Was it good theology? Or did it more nearly resemble a trinket meant for the pacification of strong desires? If so, to what extent might its useful effects (whatever they were) override its disruptive ones (whatever those might prove to be), or vice versa? These were certainly weighty questions.

The wonder, in the 1970s, was the rapidity—for that matter, the ease—with which the Episcopal Church made up its mind. In a mere decade, Episcopalians moved from official commitment to the "catholic" view of priesthood to the general, if not yet wholly successful, stubbing out of that same commitment. Once the General Convention had elected to engage the issue, the outcome was clear, at least from the standpoint of those who had come to note (some with satisfaction, others with deep apprehension) the Episcopal Church's ever-warmer embrace of cultural norms.

Yes, certainly, the church would embrace this additional step in the empowerment of the powerless. It had done so, as we have noted already, with respect to the civil rights of black Americans. It was obligated now to extend to women the same recognition of innate humanity and aspiration, or so the spirit of the time whispered insistently. The deprivation of women, who were after all a numerical majority of the population, enjoying in many cases wealth and standing, was less easy to prove than the deprivation of blacks, to which television and newspaper coverage, as well as personal experience, testified. It was enough for some proponents of women's ordination to note a coincidence that seemed more than coincidence. Who sought to keep blacks "in their place"? White males. Who benefited chiefly from patronizing and hushing up women? White males. There you were. The burgeoning culture of the time, with its inherent dislike of authority and those who appeared to profit there from, believed it had sniffed out a consequential datum about social arrangements.

For America to become "just," it was essential (so said those deeply attached to the justice question) to erase artificial distinctions among Americans. So, then, the distinction between the ministerial roles of men and women was "artificial"? It depended on how one chose to examine that distinction, whether from the standpoint of secular politics or the standpoint of traditional Christian theology. There was one more possibility. What if the Holy Spirit was speaking a new, extremely non-traditional word to the faithful? About women, about their role in the church? What if, indeed, the ear of the church had for some time been deaf to the spirit's entreaties and the time had come to set matters right?

That was how General Convention meant to, and did, address the matter. The Convention was far from offering itself as the ecclesiastical branch of the women's liberation movement. Yet the premises on which it operated bore an uncanny resemblance to those on which organized feminism operated. To wit, women *lacked*, therefore women *deserved*.

How was the trick to be pulled off? Waiting for the Spirit to reemerge as the "rushing mighty wind" of Acts 2 could take considerable time, as well as a patience no longer notable in a culture boiling with outrage over unaddressed injustices (which, indeed, not all Americans viewed as injustices). The Spirit had therefore to be given some credit for whispering all along particular things in particular ears, things about the proper, as opposed to the historic, place of women in the church. True, those who claimed to hear contrary allegations from the Spirit were due their day in court, their opportunity to cite unbroken tradition, not to mention some fairly plain words of Scripture as against the revelations others were claiming. Yet there were ways of responding without calling in Betty Friedan as an expert witness.

We reach a matter absolutely central to any consideration of the Episcopal Church's noisy, toilsome journey through modern times. The question is how a church can understand and say different things in different ages and yet in both cases be faithful to truth. Equally to the point is the question of why nowadays so many Christians *expect* the church so to behave, especially in contexts fraught with cultural and political implications.

The question is whether and how doctrine develops over time, and with what outcomes. That Christian beliefs and ideas and concepts and practices can in fact develop over time—can unfold themselves, spread out, contract, whatever the case might be—all Christians would acknowledge. Instances are endless. Whereas in the early days adult baptism for the rigorously instructed was the rule and practice, Christians long have baptized infants who rather clearly entertained no notion of regeneration and new birth through water and the Holy Ghost. What do Christians make of the Eucharist memorial? True Body and Blood, varies not only from church to church but also, I dare say, from Christian to Christian. The very intonations of Holy Scripture are bound to resound differently in different sets of ears. Do you believe the great fish gulped down Jonah? What if you do? What if you don't?

When the question of priesthood for women arose at mid-century, the authority of the Church Fathers to bind the church forever came immediately into question. The church of the apostolic age, an age of "patriarchy," had lived amid assumptions radically different from those of our own times. It was natural, was it not, for the church to assume about women roughly what the culture assumed—namely, that in every department of life, women should ask and men should answer? It was not quite a *quod erat demonstrandum*, but it advanced the argument, because in the end the argument was about creating a church better suited to the twentieth century than to the first—an age that proudly gave women jobs and suffrage rather than enjoined them to stay home and keep quiet.

The datedness of first-century ways had to be emphasized. With which consideration a problem quickly arose: to wit, if the first century had got it wrong about women, what else had it gotten wrong about beliefs, doctrines, standards, and expectations? What else needed modification, or a good deal more than modification? There was no immediate need for a full and proper accounting, but as we shall shortly see the questions would reemerge in full strength once the dispute over women as priests had been seemingly settled. For now, it sufficed that the time had come to lift the hand of the past from the strong and capable shoulders of women so that they might do what God had fitted them for.

And what was that, exactly? The church, as we have noted, had ideas on that score that were harder to brush aside than the Friedanists of the Episcopal Church were willing to acknowledge. Those ideas were not merely cultural; they incorporated an understanding having to do with *reality*, as the church had learned it during many long centuries: that which *was*, as contrasted with human appetite or will.

What did reality have to say? For one thing, it said that Christ had died for the sins of both sexes, no more so for one sex than for the other. How was *that* for "equality," in whatever way conceived? There was certainly more to the matter. It began perhaps with the recognition that there *were* two sexes, each distinct from the other. A mere commonplace? Not at all. A man was more likely than a woman to assume the role of provider for the family— not that a woman wasn't up to the task. (I recall with tenderness an oft-told family tale concerning one of my great-grandmothers, a Civil War survivor married to a woefully under-compensated school superintendent, who moved herself and their daughters to Austin and opened a boarding house, so that the girls might afford to attend the University of Texas!) Equally, just because women specialized in the duties, often enough the drudge work, of the household, was there objective reason to suppose men would fall on their faces if they attempted such tasks?

There were anatomical distinctions that signaled distinctions in function. That is, women were the incubators and deliverers of life, men the progenitors. Neither function stood by itself; rather, each complemented the other. No man could be a mother; no woman could be a father. So? Pride of place was not in the least the point. The point was the complementarity of distinct functions: the working interrelationship of abilities, along lines that every human enterprise had contrived both naturally and logically. What if, for instance, a major research university faculty comprised agronomists only? It would be hard learning history or political philosophy—or anything besides agronomy. Did the high-tech industry hire none but cybernetic experts? Were all forty-eight partners in Beatum, Cheatum & Wringum learned only in the law of liens and creditors' rights?

In its apportionment of functions—this servant of the Lord for that task, that one for another—the church reflected not only the spiritual model as laid out by St. Paul ("And his gifts were that some should be apostles, some prophets, some evangelists"), but likewise the secular model ("And the human relations office decreed that some should be lawyers, some technicians, some teachers").

It was just there that the theological model ran into trouble. What offended many was the basic premise on which the church had divided up its functions. The church excluded women from the priesthood. This would never do, inasmuch as the secular society was in the process of deciding that women should be admitted to all forms of work, including military service. What exempted the church from this prescription? If one looked at the matter, a clerical collar fit a woman's neck as easily as a man's. A woman (*pace* Dr. Johnson) could preach; a woman could make budgets, return phone calls, and visit hospitals, probably with great efficiency. Just what was there anyway a male priest could do that an inspired and dedicated woman could not?

Given the tone and temper of the times, defenders of, shall we say, the established order had their work cut out for them. Their task, bleak at best, was to show that the cause of civil rights and workplace opportunity had no bearing on the theology of the church. Moreover, the defenders of the old order were not completely at one as to the necessity of reserving the priesthood for males.

By and large it was Anglo-Catholics, scrupulous about sacramental validity, and more than a little sympathetic, truth be told, to Roman Catholic viewpoints and outlooks, who put up the strongest resistance. Much more flexible were the evangelicals, their sacramental interests and doctrinal, as opposed to biblical, concerns more relaxed than those of the Anglo-Catholics, their interest in Roman and Eastern Orthodox viewpoints (for the Orthodox, too, reserved the priesthood for males) infinitely slighter.

The evangelical passion, moreover, was for conversion to the Gospel rather than for (a trap into which Anglo-Catholics sometimes stumbled headlong) solemn, not to say picturesque, worship as central to church mission. The Episcopal evangelical might not dismiss all the theological disabilities associated in theory with the estate of womanhood. Nevertheless, a generic evangelical was more likely than a generic Anglo-Catholic to hear out with interest the case for "updating" the theology of priesthood. I might go so far as to say that evangelicals, with their easy informality and friendliness, their gift for salesmanship and innate understanding of the "customers," are more typically "American" than the Anglo-Catholics, hence likelier to blend in with the culture.

A decade later, when gay rights issues came to the fore, evangelicals would come to understand, sometimes faster than the Catholics, just what damage the culture had inflicted on the church of God. Their indignation, kindled by years of deepening stress over church events, would prove pivotal in bringing the church to confront at last the spectacle of rancor and division it had allowed, if not encouraged.

There were other dispositions within the church, none especially sympathetic to the suddenly imperiled institution of the all-male priesthood. The low churchman was the theological heir of the Reformation, ever on guard against innovations that threatened to undermine Anglican independence of Rome. Seemingly "Romish" appurtenances like fancy liturgical dress and even the use of the term "Father" to address a clergyman were, to the truly low, abhorrent—more so, maybe, than the tendency of others in the broad middle to talk more energetically of social concerns than of theological reasonings.

The "broad church" movement within Anglicanism scoured the world for secular causes to embrace as proof of the Gospel mandate to seek and effect justice—meaning, it usually turned out, the lowering or destruction of barriers between classes and kinds. Broad churchmen (a better word in the American context is "liberals") found in the 1960s no scarcity of causes to embrace, starting with civil rights for black Americans. The Episcopal "liberal" sat lightly to new ways of receiving and understanding Christian doctrine. His was not a mind "hung up" (in 1960s-speak) on the perpetuation of the obsessions of people not blessed with modern knowledge and understandings. He wished to be flexible and inquisitive at the same time. When in the 1960s the attacks began in earnest on male "privilege" within the church, an amplitude of ears listened sympathetically. Sex discrimination was the charge. Yes? What about it?

The movement to ordain women succeeded in the Episcopal Church largely because most of those who oversaw the church's affairs agreed with critics, male as well as female, who deplored "discrimination" against women. Others perhaps saw the matter as insufficiently important to become worked up about. Indifference, as we know, can serve the cause of revolutionaries as well as fierce attachment can.

Episcopalians who argued for women's rights saw their institution as connected to the divine purpose, but enchained as often as not by human perceptions, human enactments, human prejudices rooted in human history and nourished by human experience. Take "patriarchy," or rule and government by males. Was it to be assumed the patriarchal attitudes of pre-twentieth-century societies had never, anywhere, influenced Christian attitudes toward women? Of course not. Then take the church's present-day "conservatives," so critical of cultural seepage into the church, so determined to stop it. Let these pious parties deny that the assumptions of patriarchal cultures formed the attitudes of the church, and vice versa. Hard as they might try, we all knew (did we not?) the workings of culture—that great sea on which we float, the waves rocking or tossing us, salt invading mouth and nostrils until the wet and salty become the normal even, possibly, the *true*.

Well, then, here was the culture of a new day summoning us to new awareness of the disadvantages under which Christian women long had labored. Here were creatures of God, confined by tradition and custom to the opposite side of the communion rail from the priest and the bishop—except when doing "womanly" things like preparing the altar for the service or resetting hymn boards. What were Episcopalians going to do about it?

The sudden summons to equality met with some wonderment among Episcopalians unused to thinking of themselves as callous enslavers of womankind. It was likely fruitful to examine the situation of women in the church of the late twentieth century and ask vital questions about roles and capabilities. And yet the new equality gospel smelled strongly of secular places like faculty lounges, newsrooms, and lecture halls. Within the church a different gospel of equality rang out, or was supposed to—one that affirmed the essential unity of men and women in the forgiveness and mercy of Christ. If it was reasonable to castigate the church for listening too keenly to modern culture, it was likewise reasonable to ask whether the church had non-secular and particular reasons for reserving the priesthood to males.

Those who approached the question front-end first, that is, theologically instead of politically, might learn to appreciate some of the church's scruples about blurring the fundamental identities of men and of women, as bestowed in creation: man as creator, woman as keeper of that creation. Were these concepts too philosophical, too representational, for our hard-boiled, channel-flipping age? Then what of the need for the priest to represent Christ in his entire humanity, meaning, among other things, his maleness? Was that too precious a consideration for those who thought of jobs chiefly as avenues to personal fulfillment? Perhaps, though that hardly disposed of the question.

Is this to say, all the same, that such considerations make no sense apart from some imputed drive on the male's part to keep the womenfolk well and truly subservient? If, in fact, male egotism, power, and lust are the driving forces in Christian theology, much more is wrong with Christianity than can be addressed through the ordination of women as priests. Yet, if God's hand should be in this thing—which is to say, if Christians before our time read their Maker rightly and configured the priesthood in accordance with that reading—the minimum we might wish to say is, "Lord, have mercy."

The strategy of Episcopalians, pleased with the prospect of ending their church's "exclusion" of women from the seats of "power," succeeded largely by explaining away the old understandings. Times had changed. What the church formerly said it believed was a dead letter. As for the Romans and the Orthodox, who saw the old beliefs as true, well, you had to take into account their musty and authoritarian mindsets. To Episcopalians, it was Christ's humanity, not his gender (the grammatical term then beginning to replace the physiological term "sex"), that mattered. And how did we come to know this, when what we thought we knew formerly was something quite different? Assertion was the ticket: tireless repetition by the proponents of change; loud, ceaseless pounding on closed doors; all in all, the familiar mode of secular politics, if it came to that. Why not? It was the mode of the same world the church was endeavoring to address.

From the 1960s forward, amid social and cultural upheaval of a force and magnitude thitherto unknown in the United States, the mode of Episcopal leadership came more and more to resemble the mode of the radicalized culture: impatient, indignant, angry at times, given to bald, bold declarations that might or might not bear intellectual scrutiny. It was the mode of the cultural left, for instance, to engage in tirades (not to mention physical protest) against the war in Vietnam, racial injustice, and supposedly outworn moral notions. To the counterculture, as the general rebellion was called, the civilities of debate and disputation mattered infinitely less than those certainties the counterculture held in its hand. The United States *was* racist and sexist. It *was* imperialist. It *was* oppressive. Wasn't all this plain? It should have been. To see things otherwise was to engage in self-deceit.

Not that Episcopalians of all people were likely to dress in beads and bangles and thrust flowers into the muzzles of National Guardsmen's rifles, or to stalk the streets, waving angry banners. Yet the assertive style of the counterculture, with due concession to social proprieties, became the style of the church's own revolutionaries. The ecclesiastical revolutionaries might not care to fret long over the intricacies and subtleties of Eucharistic theology. One verse from the Bible, nevertheless, they recited with joyous intensity: "Behold, I make all things new"—from St. John's Revelation. Yes, new, like the ever-revolving, always evolving world! All around, there were new lifestyles, new habits, new thought patterns; one had but to put one's head out the window to find them. The world fairly vibrated with possibilities and opportunities once denied, if glimpsed at all. No more Eisenhower years of consolidation and cultural retrenchment. One could feel the rhythms of the new life: harmony and understanding, sympathy and trust abounding . . .

The Aquarians who moonlighted as members of the Episcopal Church pricked up their ears. God was doing a new thing in their midst, the Holy Spirit leading the way, the faithful fearlessly following. Along the way, old, no-longer-reliable baggage could be discarded. By electing to ordain women, the Episcopal Church chose the "prophetic" path, expecting the rightful reward of those who takes risks for—I almost said "heaven."

Not quite. The Episcopal Church's love affair with women as it imagined women to be—hurt, disrespected, excluded—reflected as much as anything else a passion to conform the church to worldly expectations of justice, fulfillment, and, of course, opportunity. From this passion at least four consequences were to follow.

The first, I am bound to acknowledge, was some significant satisfaction with the new order of things. Yes, why *not* women at the altar? To various Episcopalians, it all made sense. It was time. Things couldn't and shouldn't go on the old way. A woman priest of the Church of England has lately put the matter cogently: "I think of the pleasure felt and expressed by people of all backgrounds when they see men and women working together as colleagues in church. . . . Men-only clubs continue to have a quaint value, but the norm in church and society is men and women celebrating their complementary gifts and outlooks. . . . I think, too, of the distinctive grace that women have brought to the church. They bless people's lives with their own brand of care, for those getting married, having children, finding faith or journeying towards death."

The necessity of their performing these splendid services while wearing priestly garments never emerges in testimony of this agreeable, sometimes inspiring, sort.

If these and like experiences made up the residue of the Episcopal passion for women, that would certainly be one thing. There remain three additional consequences to examine. I am sorry to say not one of them is positive.

The second consequence is disunion, the deliberate severing of ancient bonds. The church, with minimal discussion or preparation, had chosen a new way. What of those Episcopalians who held sincerely to the old way? Too bad for them. A line had been drawn in the sand. Those unwilling to cross it had been declared, in effect, back numbers, if not indeed "sexists." Poor souls! Could they not hear the Spirit's promptings? Their General Convention not only had heard, but had responded. It remained for Episcopal recusants to conform their minds and spirits to the new program—or else.

There was certainly one answer for such a challenge, a very American one: Leave. Hardly had General Convention executed its great leap forward before Anglo-Catholics began peeling off from the Church. The idea was to remain Anglican, outside an Episcopal Church whose sacraments were at best doubtful on account of the admission to the priesthood of candidates unfitted by nature, in a way for which no one could blame them, to become priests of the church. Those who withdrew from the church saw themselves as "continuing" a heritage General Convention had bagged up and left for the trash man—hence their name for themselves, the "continuing churches," with localized names like the Province of Christ the King, the American Anglican Church, the Anglican Church in America, or the Anglican Rite Jurisdiction of the Americas, each one, however tiny, with its own set of bishops. They, not their ex-Episcopalian brethren, represented (as they saw it) the church unpolluted by compromise with the standards and teachings of the world.

There was something redolent of Protestantism in the Catholic determination to withdraw from fellowship with the otherwise-minded—to take their theology elsewhere and hold it close. Yet the Catholics had a point. What if, in fact, the Episcopal Church, by doing something new and doubtful, had scuttled its claim to be a church of sacraments? If a woman priest was no priest, her theological actions—blessing, pardoning, mediating the mysterious transformation of bread and wine into the Body and Blood of Christ—were actions only, lacking theological content. The Episcopalian sitting still for such ministrations might as well be sitting in a Quaker meeting hall for all the spiritual benefit he derived.

The "continuers," few as they were numerically, represented a large loss to the church, in fervor as well as in devotion to the belief that the Christian faith was a reality that proceeded from the mind and will of God. Not all Catholics left. In some cases entire dioceses (e.g., Fort Worth, Texas; San Joaquin, California; Quincy, Illinois) declined either to ordain women as priests or to receive as priests women ordained elsewhere. Most evangelicals and low churchmen found women priests who knew their Bible (and many did) acceptable additions to the clergy. Still other Anglican provinces—including the mother church, the Church of England—followed Episcopal promptings and shortly voted to ordain women. Was this not confirmation of the Spirit's promptings? What was unity, after all, at the cost of infidelity to the will of God, as whispered discreetly to the General Convention of the Episcopal Church?

It is well worth noting that the shuffle of departing Catholic feet woke up others to the possibility of escape. If the Catholics could leave, why not those for whom issues such as scriptural authority and gay rights were paramount? Through large doors left ajar by departing critics of women's ordination, many left behind could now see sunlight. It was not only respectable to move apart from false teachers—it was vital. Souls were at risk! A church proud of its part in flipping upside down an ancient teaching about priesthood was sure to find new ways of putting distance between itself and the historic faith. Could such a church feel shame or regret over rewriting the moral law? The sunlight streaming through the open church door beckoned with new urgency to Episcopalians fearful of a leadership disposed to pronounce all forms of "loving" sexual activity valid in God's sight.

The third consequence of the General Convention's lurch into the arms of a new theory of priesthood was pure exhilaration, large-eyed wonder and delight at the ease with which major transformation, once undertaken, could be achieved. *Prove* the case for change? Why? Always there would be those deaf to the new truths the spirit was speaking. To wait and pray for consensus would be to evade a sacred responsibility, that of *acting*. In the end, the priesthood of women was "true" because the General Convention of the Episcopal Church decided that an idea as good as the wider inclusion of women in church affairs simply *had* to be true, never mind the naysayers. Everyone knew, surely, how naysayers never affirmed, always demanding instead to know the causes and proofs of a new assertion. Their archetype was the old Virginia Anglican John Randolph of Roanoke, who had made it "a cardinal principle of statesmanship" never—save in the most urgent circumstances—"to disturb a thing that is at rest." As the new generation of Episcopal leaders saw things, the assertions of dead people might be interesting; they might even to some extent be clarifying. But dispositive? No, hardly that anymore. Behold, the Lord made "all things new." An easy habit, that, to get into—going with the cultural flow; taking inspiration from the newspapers and the internet, as opposed to the scriptures and a long tradition of thought and meditation.

The fourth consequence was more momentous yet. It flowed—rapidly, headlong—from the second, third, and fourth. It involved the deliberate diversion of historic Christian assumptions into new channels of thought and understanding. A certain kind of woman had to be given her way. She had to be set at liberty to reconstruct Christian reality and fit it for a new kind of world, one in which no man was going to get away with assumptions of "patriarchal superiority," and in which a long record of injustice to women would be redressed. A Day of Jubilee was in store for the church—if men, for a change, would just keep their mouths shut.

That was the hard-line view of things, to be sure. Not all Episcopal women by any means sought the power to give Christianity an explicitly feminine—or feminist—twist. I must interject here that I know women priests of profound spirituality, profoundly respectful of the ancient faith of the church—at least, those portions of the faith unassociated with job credentials. Such women stand far, far apart from the kind of woman who sees herself as part of a vast sisterhood at war with "sexism" as practiced and preached throughout Christendom.

Many a "war of liberation" had commenced during the 1960s. Here was another. Women of the church claimed the titles and charters denied them by self-seeking, suspicious males. "Feminism," said the Roman Catholic theologian Rosemary Radford Ruether, "claims that *women too* are among those oppressed whom God comes to vindicate and liberate." An obvious part of liberation was the assumption of opportunities long withheld: jobs, preferments, or the right of a woman to become presiding bishop of the Episcopal Church. There was more. Christianity's sexist orientation had to go: that is, Christianity as a system (according to the Episcopal theologian Carter Heyward, a woman despite her Christian name) devoted to "men's domination and women's submission . . . a movement to repress those uppity women and men who have dared to resist sexual and gender control."

How was liberation to be achieved? The ordination of women as priests was the merest beginning, an essential first step but hardly the last. A vital part of the new understanding was the squelching of the notion of a patriarchal God with a long beard, a favorer of males. The feminists pressed their audiences for supposedly clarifying language about God. Some took to identifying Him as "Father/Mother God," or, still more radically, "she." Or just plain "God," the better to avoid pronouns.

Well, wait. Had not God identified Himself as Father, King, and Lord? Yes, but look: That was the patriarchalist way of talking. A non-"male" God? The Church couldn't imagine such, any more than we formerly could imagine a female Supreme Court justice or banker or astronaut. The new, remodeled Christian community would henceforth shed its male appurtenances and prejudices. It would be tolerant of diversity, remembering as it did its own record of oppression. It would stress, as Carter Heyward put it, "mutuality as a vital life-force that is the substance of love, friendship, and voluntary cooperation at all levels of human engagement." The God whom Heyward wished to affirm "is the God of relation and friendship . . . God of justice for the poor . . . justice for women . . . justice for the outcast and 'the other' . . . and God of sexuality . . . .I have no interest, except an angry one, in an 'otherworldly' God who sets 'Himself' above and against human suffering, work, play, sexuality, doubt, humor, questions, physicality, and material needs."

A God, if you look closely, rather like the God of Orthodox Christianity, thoroughly engaged with the world and its concerns. Only not on Heyward's ideological terms. That would be the real difficulty in the search for a God of whom they approved. The God of whom they might approve is, in Christian terms, there already, obscured only by the verbal smokescreens of those who demand He instantly come forth and agree with *them.*

Such is the volume and the vigor of the feminist theologians that their influence is easy to overestimate. I doubt most Episcopalians have so much as *heard* of Carter Heyward, much less identified themselves with her arraignment of the "patriarchalist" God. Equally it would be a mistake to see her influence as merely exotic. We have noted at some length how the Episcopal Church deliberately accommodated the clamor for "jobs" once reserved for men. Consider the effects of admitting to positions of influence in the church such women, not to mention such men, as sip or gulp the Heywardian view of God, or the resemblances to it infiltrating the church from outside.

The prayer book of 1979 commenced the still incomplete work of "de-sexing" the worship forms through which Episcopalians imbibe their theology, disposing deftly, where it could, of "man," "mankind," and "sons." The revisers, who left untouched such familiar attestations as "Lord" and "Father, Son, and Holy Spirit," slashed at the Psalter, nevertheless, with feminist zeal, inserting "gender-neutral" language in place of the old, supposedly misrendered patriarchalist forms.

Note Psalm 1 in the old version: "Blessed is the man that hath not walked in the counsel of the ungodly." Then note the same Psalm as rendered in the 1979 book: "Happy are *they* who have not walked in the counsel of the wicked." Out with "man," notwithstanding the word's historic status as indicative of both sexes. As with the prayer book, so with the hymnal that emerged three years later; "gender-specific" language was pruned, even in familiar texts like "Hark, the Herald Angels Sing." No more the alliteration and euphony of "pleased as Man with man to dwell." More to the point—the feminist point—is "pleased as man with us to dwell."

The revisers' sense was that, liturgically speaking, familiarity breeds comfort or, anyway, resignation. The same understanding animates the secular writers and publishers and editors working more or less successfully to scrub ordinary secular usage of its maleness. As a onetime college teacher of writing, I defy anyone to find more than a handful of college students who recognize instinctively, and with some aversion, the gaffe involved in "Everybody has their book"! Meanwhile, the New Revised Standard Version of the Bible blots up traces of linguistic sexism wherever it finds them, never mind the "sexism" of the original language.

I don't think anyone would assert darkly that "pleased as man with us to dwell" paves the descent to Hell. We might better regard a phrase of this sort (and there are many such) as linguistic Novocain, deadening the nerves against deeper drilling into the Christian corpus, drilling intended to expose unsuspected ideas, understandings, doctrines, and truths. All who see religion as an evolving project—never firm, never fixed, always seeking, always moving—are elated by the search, even more so as creaky establishments like the Episcopal Church join in the search with zeal. The bill, nevertheless, could prove a high one: the collapse of orthodox Christianity into the form of a blanket affording generic affirmation instead of highly non-affirming truth. The Episcopal Church has not overhauled its liturgy since 1979, but there are afoot projects likely to succeed in the near future, such as the diminution of references to Jesus' rather regrettable, if undeniable, maleness.

A feminist specific for this complaint is the blind eye. Thus, as substitute for the historic Trinitarian formula—Father, Son, and Holy Ghost (or Spirit)—increasingly we hear feminists, inside and outside the Episcopal Church, speaking of God as "Creator, Redeemer, Sustainer." All a matter of function and activity, then, this Trinitarian business? Nothing to do with identity? Modalism, an ancient Christian heresy, traversed similar ground and got itself roundly condemned. The fathers of the church could be counted on to swat away every suggestion of divine diversity, of God carved into discrete slices like the deities of Canaan and no more worthy of worship than they.

On an adjacent front in the linguistic battle, Carter Heyward finds value in use of the pronoun "she" for God, partly "to compensate in tiniest measure for the overwhelming extent to which the deity remains 'he' in Christian tradition," and partly because "womanpower" is "a resource of profound spiritual transformation."

Things could be worse. Roman Catholicism seems sometimes to have it roughest in terms of the interaction it receives from the likes of Mary Daly, whose barely comprehensible views, derived in part from her commitment to lesbianism, push theological radicalism to the edge. Contends Elizabeth Achtemeir, of Union Theological Seminary in Richmond, Virginia: "There can be no doubt that feminist theologians are in the process of laying the foundations for a new faith and a new church that are, at best, only loosely related to apostolic Christianity . . . many women, in their dedication to the feminist movement, are being slowly wooed into a new form of religion, widely at variance with the Christian faith . . . the unwary and the unknowing are led astray, and the Body of Christ suffers for it."

She notes further: "Feminism has invaded the realm of God, and in some instances, the God of the Christian faith has been replaced with a god or goddess of the feminists' making. . . . The fathers have eaten sour grapes, and the daughters' teeth are set on edge." Carter Heyward might well nod vigorously in agreement. As she has noted, "I am re-imaging God and Jesus in order to speak my truth." *Her* truth. We do well to note that frank admission.

And so the re-invention, re-tooling, re-working, and re-amplification of Christianity goes forward, often without notice to the body of Christ called the Church. We are used to women priests. They no longer amaze us. How long before the exotic theology of some ceases also to amaze us? Is "truth," after all, a chimerical notion, a will-o'-the-wisp, changing forms from time to time and place to place, imparting new understandings the church must ever be at pains to grasp? If that is so, maybe no one can say any longer, or would want to say, what guidelines, what decencies, what norms and standards fit all cases.

There's of course an obvious problem here. Not just two, but many, can play at such a game. Can and *do*—and not necessarily to the enrichment of Christian witness.

EIGHT ～
Sex, Anyone?

T HE GREEK MYTH OF PANDORA AND HER BOX STILL FASCINATES
and beguiles: Woman—I suppose it could equally have been
man, but we know these old Attic patriarchalists, don't we?—opens
forbidden container, and out into the world swarm all manner of
slimy, cringe-making evils.

The difficulty with applying Pandora's story to modern times,
perhaps to any given age, is the implication that a single action
is capable of producing all the disorder in the air. Events have
roots; roots have shoots: We have covered this ground already.
I retrace it only for the sake of emphasizing the anarchic quality
of late-twentieth-century life, a happy anarchy of which the Episcopal Church happily partook when it elected to ordain women
as priests, and which it never thereafter forsook.

Was women's ordination the Episcopal Pandora's box? Not
really. The Episcopal style, theologically speaking, was already by
the early 1970s loose and accommodating. A more uptight—that
favorite 1960s reproach—institution would have handily beaten
back the loudest demands for change. The Episcopal Church was

anything but uptight by this stage, least of all, perhaps, in questions of sex.

In the 1970s, the relatively rigorous moral standards of yore, as to male-female relationships, had for a long time been in decay. Perhaps Freud started it, and, again, perhaps not. Any yearning as strong as that of one human for another involves sacrifice, mortification, anguish, betrayal, death. Small wonder to find love's pathway heavily staked with cautions, warning signs, exhortations, regulations, most of them produced over long centuries with the aid of religious insight and wisdom. The Christian church's mission to guide, insofar as possible, the course of true and sometimes turbulent love was part and parcel of its mission to strengthen the whole community as its members established lives together, and homes, and then brought children into the world. The trouble was that, as the twentieth century lurched along, fewer and fewer wished the church's guidance, or, perhaps more to the point, took that guidance seriously. What growing numbers wished for was a certain latitude to make moral decisions by intuition or perceived need, if not whim, outside the light that moral prescriptions had traditionally thrown on human affairs.

In Anglican life those moral prescriptions had their most vivid form in the language of the Book of Common Prayer. We have noted how the English prayer book of 1662 taught bluntly "the causes for which Matrimony was ordained." Allow me to come back to this stout old prescription. First, marriage was for "the procreation of children; then it provided "a remedy against sin, and to avoid fornication"; lastly, it afforded "the mutual society, help, and comfort, that the one [partner] ought to have of the other, both in prosperity and adversity." This was austere, to say the least: quite colorless and self-abnegating. No fun in it—that is, no fun in the jolly, riotous sense that participants in the twenty-first century's matrimonial rites would recognize. .

The new Protestant Episcopal Church of the post-revolutionary period, perhaps with a sense of relief, excised from the prayer book this candid explanation without modifying the basic understanding of marriage as a solemn event, heavy with theological meaning and summonses to duty. It was "instituted of God, signifying unto us the mystical union that is betwixt Christ and his Church: which holy estate Christ adorned and beautified with his presence and first miracle that he wrought in Cana of Galilee," and so was "not by any to be entered into unadvisedly or lightly; but reverently, discreetly, advisedly, soberly, and in the fear of God." Stout stuff, yes, reflecting a large and serious view of a human institution joined through and through to the high purposes of the Creator.

"The Form of Solemnization of Matrimony" was the title of the old marriage service—a testimony to what the church saw as happening in the solemn exchange of solemn vows. On page 423 of the 1979 prayer book, a new name and focus appeared: "The Celebration and Blessing of a Marriage." In the new name was more than a hint of what the modern church thought it was hearing in the streets outside—exuberance, vivacity, merriment, all things the old Puritans certainly wouldn't have known about or approved of if they had.

True to their calling, the revisers painted out all the dark language they could, lightening tone and mood. Their ears had deceived them, and not just in a literary sense. Those cultural celebrations they believed themselves to have heard, and responded to, were in fact rendings and tearings; the sounds of Christian marriages coming to grief on the rocks of dissatisfaction, restlessness, and anger. America's divorce culture was undergoing birth throes. Nor was the Episcopal Church finding much to say amid the tumult.

It was all so very modern! We earlier noted, with Frederick Lewis Allen's aid, the uncoiling of old inhibitions—the fears, doubts, and anxieties, that supposedly held back full expression of . . . we might call it personhood. There had been shortened hemlines and bobbed hair and rumble-seat sex. And, no, an older generation hadn't liked it, but what of that? A younger, freer generation had liked it very much indeed. ("Millions of people were moving toward acceptance of what a *bon-vivant* of earlier days had said was his idea of the proper state of morality—'A single standard, and that a low one.'") All this implied the assertion of individual will, inevitably, in many cases, over against the expectations of others, and even the solemn undertakings stipulated in the prayer book rite: "until death do us part" and all that.

By 1928, the divorce rate—a mere 8.8 per hundred marriages in 1910—had nearly doubled, reaching 16.5 percent. It cannot be denied that some of these shattered unions had probably not been mutual blessings to begin with, but the fact remained that Christianity not merely esteemed matrimony but saw it as that "holy estate" mentioned in the prayer book.

Things were to get worse yet. The great loosenings—plural—of the 1960s profoundly affected ideas about family structure and authority and, on that account, the human laws that regulated such matters. Thanks to Betty Friedan, but much more to the cultural spirit that had given authority to her notions, a woman enjoyed the right to dissatisfaction with the satisfactions promised her. Further, she had a right to seek alternative satisfactions. That meant freer access to divorce. For that matter, men, who were after all 50 percent of the marital arrangement, enjoyed like rights.

State legislatures, duly responsive to popular will, hastened to satisfy the demand. Between 1967 and 1975, a breathtakingly narrow window, "no fault" divorce laws swept America. A couple could divorce merely by being willing to divorce. More than just the stuff of old-fashioned farce—private detectives snooping around hotels to catch one spouse or the other *in flagrante*—disappeared. The sense of permanent commitment to marriage disappeared also. Mere "incompatibility" was now a pretext for the sundering of supposedly sacred unions: Never mind what promises the incompatible pair might have made to each "in the sight of God, and in the face of this Company."

William J. Bennett's *Index of Leading Cultural Indicators* informs us that whereas in 1960 there had been 73.5 marriages and 9.2 divorces for every married female, the mid-1990s brought corresponding rates of 55.7 and 21. Likewise, the percentage of children living with divorced parents soared from 2.1 percent in 1960 to 9.5 percent thirty years later. As social stigmas associated with divorce began to wane, extramarital sex and cohabitation acquired protective armament, if not quite cachet. The saga of sexual liberation was retailed by every minstrel singer who could be recruited to glorify human choice and the disappearance of artificial social restraints, not least in that new freedom conferred by the United States Supreme Court in 1973—the freedom in most if not all circumstances to abort an unborn baby. The extent to which *Roe* v. *Wade* swayed cultural attitudes about sex has not to my knowledge been adequately chronicled, nor can it be chronicled here. Suffice it, perhaps, to say that the sudden gift of power over human life, in however limited a sphere, was a heady thing, a prerogative once reserved for kings, now (in a democratic age) distributed almost universally.

Children might be the gift of God Himself, but as things stood from 1973 forward, grown men and women could spare the Donor the trouble of further gifts, or could instruct Him concerning their preferred timetables. An atmosphere of this sort, it goes without saying, breathes little reverence. It goes without saying also that in such an atmosphere even the guardians of reverence—bishops, priests, theologians—are likely to scratch their heads, wondering whether the world has turned upside down.

It would seem to depend: the present world or the world beyond all worlds? By the standards of the world of eternity, the Episcopal Church seemed obligated to defend and promote—even against the inclinations of the age—whatever was God's, drawing wisdom and resolve from past struggles against the present world's inclinations while preaching to that world a message of repentance and redemption. It was a message for which the Episcopal Church showed less and less aptitude as time passed.

I recess the matter of sex and commitment for a moment only in order to draw the camera farther back.

The waters were heady in those times. Everyone acknowledged as much, not least those priests and bishops, joined by a significant company of laity, who had drunk deeply of those waters. From the time of Bishop James A. Pike, new insights from the world had beguiled the Episcopal Church. The church of the 1950s thirsted for a more vivid role in daily life, a role involving risk and no small degree of adjustment to evolving realities. Pike had in certain respects been a bit of a nut. He embraced spiritualism, became an alcoholic and an adulterer. Ultimately he abandoned his calling as a Christian priest. But he had amply demonstrated how the church might claim the world's attention, namely, by noticing, and then addressing, in an entertainingly serious way, the world's concerns.

Even before civil rights had stepped to center stage in national affairs, Pike had sensed or imagined—possibly both—a cultural restlessness. His nicely attuned ear appeared, like that of a dog, to pick up sounds not all in the church could hear. There was, for instance, the sound out there in the country of feet shuffling and noses twitching just when so many cups seemed ready to overflow with blessing. His ear caught also distant murmurs of admiration from a world grateful to hear (as St. Paul said of first-century Athens) "a new thing." Pike was the man to tell such a thing, and to bask in the applause. The point here, even so, is not to portray poor nutty Jim Pike as the herald of the Episcopal Church's future. The point is to note that his path became in time the path of the church whose assumptions he had sought with such obvious and mischievous delight to unsettle.

The calling of Bishop Pike, and of the mini-Pikes who steered their boat in his large wake, was to exalt liberation. The secular culture was providing adequate inspiration for the task: first, the gyrations of Elvis Presley and the musical acrobatics of Little Richard; then civil rights sit-ins; then protests in the streets against the war in Vietnam; then the hippie drug culture, the Hare Krishnas, the Weathermen, the casts of *Hair* and *Oh! Calcutta!* stripping off their clothes on stage and middle-class women burning their brassieres to protest oppression; and the Manson Family, Tiny Tim, the Black Panthers, *Easy Rider*, "Power to the People," Janis Joplin and her Southern Comfort. And everywhere choice and freedom, if not of the variety vetted by the signers of the Declaration of Independence, everywhere the cessation of rules and prohibitions and restraints and taboos and norms.

And it came to pass that what James A. Pike had heard, his church began to hear as well, and to believe.

The Episcopal Church's engagement with human liberation grew naturally out of the diligent attention its authorities (not to insult them with such a prehistoric term) were paying to groups they believed excessively deprived by American culture. As we have noted, the first group—indeed deprived by American culture—was blacks; the second notable group—less visibly deprived but infinitely more visible in Episcopal circles—was women. There was discovered eventually a third group—gays. Of this group I will speak later.

I have related already most of what there is to relate concerning the Episcopal Church's honorable engagement with the American descendants of African slaves. This is because that engagement, in the most recent times, has been mainly rhetorical: stock denunciations of "racism" mixing with stock calls for the greater inclusion of blacks in positions of Episcopal authority. To the claims of black Episcopalians for general inclusion practically all Episcopalians have acceded with good cheer, if not outright thankfulness for the disappearance of distinctions alien to a proper Christian spirit.

If anything, the Episcopal Church of the twenty-first century cultivates a passion for beating the dead horse of "racism," an animal slaughtered long ago in the church's own pasture but constantly suspected of popping up again somewhere. The latest General Convention entertained a proposal to apologize for the Episcopal Church's imputed role in the maintenance of slavery and to suggest the possibility of reparations in some unspecified amount. Desmond Tutu, the retired South African archbishop and Nobel Peace Prize winner, is among the great celebrities in Episcopal circles, a man for whom no encomium is too high, no honor too imposing. Yet, with blacks ensconced in positions of influence throughout American life—in politics, business, education, literature, and entertainment—the stock of reparative deeds available to the Episcopal Church has shrunk dramatically.

The real action in the church, in human liberation terms, moved long ago from race to sex. The role of women in the church was a crucial aspect of the whole. A no less crucial aspect was the process of—what to call it?—moral adjustment in light of all we now knew women to deserve. Yes, yes, women had the right to become priests, and what a glorious, overdue right it was! But another right, immense and shapeless, attached to their new estate. It was the right of women to define themselves—their individual identities, their who-ness and what-ness, free of others' expectations, free of the moral horse-collars society had affixed to their necks. A woman could—*should*—make up her own mind on important questions. And so, went the obvious if less-spoken implication, could a man. We were going to have freedom around here at last, lots and lots of freedom. The world was going to be a very different kind of place.

Granted, not all Americans—that included American women—desired liberation on these spacious terms. What was wrong with the old truths? Had they not guided our footsteps in a sufficiently trustworthy fashion? Was it that they had grown out of date? Anything but that, replied millions. Neither human nature nor the reality of sin had abated its impact on that package of contradictions known as the human personality. For all that, something called liberation was in the air. You never could tell who would breathe it in. It could be a churchman of serious mien just as well as it could be a college freshman with shoulder-length hair.

And often as not, seemingly, it was. For the moral upheavals of the 1960s the Episcopal Church was not wholly unprepared. No one ever had confused Episcopalians with Southern Baptists, or confused them for long, anyway. A church given to defining itself as broadly accommodating (within limits, naturally), ready to consider if not necessarily adopt new points of view, indisposed to prowling in search of ideas to swat down—such a church was unlikely to view with alarm some new thing on the mere ground of its newness. The Episcopal Church would want to look first and see what was afoot. It would seek to understand. Such was the Episcopal way.

To be sure, Episcopalians had never before encountered a tempest like the one that began to blow through America around 1960. The moral questions being raised were extraordinary even by the extraordinary standards of the 1920s. How could anyone say automatically that unmarried sex was a bad thing? And fidelity, was *that*, after all, so great a treasure? Wasn't something called "love" the main thing, especially as contrasted with hatred or even boredom in love long since expired? Love could grow; it also could shrink. How dare religion not recognize both possibilities? Why the superior state that marriage enjoyed in society? When a daughter brought her boyfriend home for the weekend, why should not both occupy her bedroom—as they did anyway during the week? What about natural and pure expression? What about love as a perpetual quest rather than a mere picket-fenced, gingham-aproned destination? As a discerning seventeenth-century Anglican, Sir Thomas Browne, had noted, "vicious times invert the opinions of things, and set up new ethics against virtue."

The moral questions ricocheting loudly around the country and society needed old answers much more, perhaps, than new ones, inasmuch as the old ones addressed matters (e.g., fidelity) conscientiously worked out over centuries and agreeable with laws long believed to be written on the heart. Yet it was new answers that church spokesmen seemed to keep producing, consonant with what journalists and publicists were beginning to call "the New Morality"—new in its concern for divorcing action from dry abstraction.

The Rev. Joseph Fletcher, whose *Situation Ethics: The New Morality*, published in 1966, became one of the decade's most famous texts, with its repudiation of legalism and "codified conduct" as artifacts of a civilization gone with the wind. Fletcher, a professor of social ethics at the Episcopal Theology School in Cambridge, Massachusetts, claimed to put people, rather than "things," at the "center of concern." He worked, that is, not from norms but supposedly from "experience." He was a relativist, the common posture of the day, as he understood it. "Our thought forms are relativistic to a degree that our forefathers never imagined." There was yet a norm, *agape*—meaning love, open-armed, abounding, compassionate. Always we were to act in love, according to "our own *responsible* estimate of the situation."

Further, we were to shun "stern, iron-bound do's and don'ts," along with "prescribed conduct and legalistic morality." It followed, if love was the guide, that love would sometimes produce moral outcomes other than those indicated by the norms. "What is to be done in any situation depends on the case, and the solution of any moral issue is, therefore, quite relative. What is right is revealed in the facts." It was a dynamic code, so to speak, for a dynamic age: ever-unfolding, ever-branching off into the forest to disclose unsuspected wonders. Fletcher's twentieth-century Americanism was to be glimpsed in the confession (boast?) of his debt to the pragmatic tradition exemplified by William James and John Dewey, wherein, as James put it, "Ideas become true just so far as they help us to get into satisfactory relations with other parts of our experience."

Fletcher—an extremely clear narrator, I should add—was not the only Anglican situationist, as probably can be well imagined. There was, inevitably, Jim Pike, ready to consecrate, if not to appropriate, practically any interesting innovation. Pike's *You and the New Morality*, which followed *Situation Ethics* by a year, reached the same conclusions, if more breezily: "It becomes obvious that there is no way to build a standard set of answers for the young—or for anyone." So did the English bishop John A. T. Robinson, in his compact and controversial treatise on the spirit of the new age, *Honest to God.* "Whatever the pointers of the law to the demands of love," said Robinson, "there can for the Christian be no 'packaged' moral judgments—for persons are more important than 'standards.'"

Or so it seemed to the situationists, who had at least, as Fletcher noted, a notable pedigree: elements of Paul Tillich, Rudolf Bultmann, Emil Brunner, G. E. Moore, Alfred North Whitehead, Dietrich Bonhoeffer, and the Niebuhrs, Reinhold and Richard, mingling on their pages. It was not only possible but to a degree inevitable in the 1960s to suppose that this was how intelligent people thought, inasmuch as this was how the intellectual establishment of the country tended to talk. So could the experience be downright pleasurable. To read the situationists, or, likelier, just to read about them, was now and then to experience a glimmer of—would "opportunity" be the word?

The old rules were off. Rules in general were off, in the church, increasingly, as in the larger society, where protesters and hippies and black militants and militant feminists were chasing frightened authority figures down corridors and boulevards. The doors of the moral cellblocks in which the old moral theologians had tried, though rarely with vast success, to enclose society's lesser appetites had been flung open, and sunshine streamed in. One could walk abroad now. In love, said the situationists. Yes, but what was "love"?—as Burt Lancaster, playing Elmer Gantry in the 1960 movie, was wont to inquire rhetorically as he warmed up a new object of desire. "Love" was for Elmer "the morning and the evening star" and a few other things as well. A nice enough line, perhaps, but no more precise than most definitions of the word. The situationists bade their pupils *work* at the task of acting on the basis of love. It was a considerable assignment, especially when it was to be carried out in a darkened bedroom or under the influence of the grape.

Nor did situationism always respond to the realities of human nature, as the old dead theologians had observed and commented on them. An element of that nature which the church had held constantly before its members, in preaching and in creeds, was the proclivity to sin—as manifested throughout Holy Writ, beginning with the disastrous encounter of the first man and first woman with a talking snake.

Ah, but that Adam and Eve narrative (as many were bound to put in)—you see, it was so very . . . so very what? Fantastic? *Fictional?* What about in its account of the iron tendency of created man and woman to seek personal satisfaction at the expense of God's will for his creations? God's will known as "the moral law"? Suppose Adam and Eve to have been types—of ourselves—and their disobedience to God's explicit command achingly typical of our modus operandi. It might be possible, in our own enlightened time, to reason out the "loving" response to a particular, as distinguished from a general, situation. Yet, given the well-known facts of human existence—war, murder, rapine, adultery, and robbery, for starters—do generous and satisfactory outcomes seem to anyone, situationists included, foreordained?

It was not easy even to ask such questions in the 1960s, far less so to answer them. The whole of the social order (a concept not likely agreeable to the situationists, that of "order") seemed to be flying apart. Kipling's Gods of the Copy-Book Headings might limp forward to explain a few points concerning human immutabilities, but with a war in Southeast Asia and ceaseless turmoil of one kind or another in the cities and the streets, and a sense of doom gathering over the land, the gods had to compete fiercely for attention. In the end, the situationists beat the traditionalists horse, foot, and dragoons.

There was never among Episcopalians a Battle of Waterloo, but there were skirmishes to show that the Fletchers, Pikes, and Robinsons had won decisively. For instance, in 1973, the church changed its canon law to countenance, in particular situations (as we might call them), the divorce and remarriage of members, even of clergy, all this notwithstanding the strong admonitions of the old prayer book. That book, not coincidentally, was then enjoying its last days as the church's official liturgy. When the Supreme Court, also in 1973, legitimized abortion as a moral choice, the Episcopal Church found little to say in response, and virtually nothing to say about the presumptive immorality involved in "terminating" a pregnancy. The situationists had come to depend on the exercise of "responsible" choice in situations of all sorts— including, it had to be presumed, the deliberate extinction of life. Perhaps the claims of an unborn child were after all "relative" to the instincts of the child's mother?

As the strains and stresses of the 1970s, 1980s, and 1990s split apart growing numbers of families—Episcopal families among them—and stranded millions of children in "single-parent homes," the Episcopal Church offered little in the way of reproach or guidance. Certainly the church rang no steeple bells, summoning listeners from far and near to help extinguish, not just a cultural, but also, a theological menace. More often than not, the modern church seemed and seems to see the crisis of the American family as a matter of marginal concern to an institution firmly wedded, as it were, to the ideal of gentle affirmation of "responsible" choice.

Of more than marginal interest in this context, I think, is the story of the Rev. Joseph Fletcher's intellectual journey in the years after *Situation Ethics.* Let him tell the story himself: "Even though I was a theologian, I was never, in fact, a religious man and never pretended to be. I never had a religious experience and never wanted one, not even half-heartedly . . . and now I am no longer a believing man either . . . In me the desire to believe—the wish, the will—just slipped away, almost imperceptibly."

The archpriest of situation ethics had moved on to a new situation? Leaving Christians to puzzle out what part of all he had told them still made sense? When one thought the thing over, it was Joseph Fletcher's abandonment of the church of the Living God that alone, perhaps, was intelligible.

NINE
Gay Times

JUST HERE WE MIGHT PAUSE FOR A BACKWARDS LOOK AT THE ground we have traversed.

What do we see? We see first the Episcopal Church embracing the cause of black civil rights in a way consistent not only with constitutional imperatives but also with, much nearer the theological point, the call of the Risen Savior to minister to all for whom He died.

There is more. We note the rubble and ruin from the cultural earthquakes of the 1960s and 1970s. We watch Episcopal clergy—energized, it might be, by the success of the crusade against segregation—starting to assail long-familiar norms and standards, asking aloud which institutions, in addition to Jim Crow, merit frontal attack.

We see the church postulating in its worship and ministry new norms of "inclusion" and "equality" that overshadow older norms. We find Episcopalians concluding that the new-old cause of women's rights demonstrates the need for leaping over all objections to the ordination of women as priests, and for seeing even the traditional understandings of the marital relationship as deserving significant expansion.

We see, in short, a grave, grand old church scurrying busily around, trying to figure out what the culture suddenly is demanding, and how to respond, rather than trying to impart to the culture its own special understanding of what matters, and why, and what Christians should if possible do in reverent obedience.

Who is one bit surprised at this point, looking about and finding the Episcopal Church grappling mightily with the question of gays and their place within the church, the precise question that for so many, within and without the church, seems to define the church? Are we pro-gay? Anti-gay? Somewhere in between? Unsure? Indifferent? The one thing I can confidently say we are *not* is indifferent. We understand that, extraordinarily enough, a question barely at the boundary of general consciousness thirty years ago has assumed central importance to the present life and future of the Episcopal Church.

Nor, apparently, do we Episcopalians know quite what to do about it—apart, I mean, from impeaching each other's convictions, sometimes affixing to each other names unbecoming in a Christian context. That may be inevitable, given the crucial nature of sexuality in human affairs. Yet the whole controversy, richly advertised in news accounts everywhere, saddens, even while it depletes the church's never-perhaps-large-enough store of missionary zeal.

Midway through the first decade of the twenty-first century, the question of what the church owes gays and what gays owe the church threatened to blow the church itself to fragments.

The consecration, in 2003, of Gene Robinson as bishop of New Hampshire brought to the fore an issue that had flared intermittently for years without unduly damaging *most* Episcopalians' *general* commitment to the church. So general was this general commitment that the generality of church leaders appear to have reasoned that one more tweak of existing arrangements in the gay rights matter either would pass without incident or would visit on the church mere collateral damage. Neither expectation proved valid. The effect of General Convention's consent to Robinson's election, and of his subsequent consecration as bishop, was that of a buzz fan knocked over into a bathtub. Shock was immense and universal. Suddenly everyone saw how things stood. Proponents of the gay rights agenda within the church could scarcely conceal—not that they tried very hard—their elation and sense of a turning point safely passed. Opponents of the gay rights agenda cannot have been altogether surprised to see a consistent warning of theirs finally, and miserably, fulfilled. Yet, as we know, it is one thing to warn, quite another to see the warning itself take on flesh and stature. From the "traditionalist" standpoint, the Robinson consecration was the ecclesiastical version of Ft. Sumter. The long-looked-for day of reckoning had dawned.

Not without cause has the Lutheran theologian Helmut Thielecke called homosexuality "a complicated and basically insoluble problem." The tale to be told here is an especially complicated and tangled one, with no sure ending in sight. Yet from it, if we look and listen with care, we may learn much about the modern world's operations on our thought patterns as a church, and on our capacity for making decisions in the light of Providence. Whatever our perspectives on the question, there is no ducking it, no hiding, no fleeing.

We seem to know more about homosexuality than ever before in history. In some sense we also know less. We know more because of the very visible efforts of the gay rights movement to achieve full incorporation into the American—for that matter, the Western—"mainstream." We know less because the gay rights movement, which began unofficially when patrons in 1969 resisted a police raid on a New York City gay bar, has unsettled common understandings about human sexuality, which is to say, about the basic purposes of men and women as the creatures of God.

Up until the 1960s and 1970s, the consensus view was that homosexuality was an inferior, if not indeed a disordered, sexual mode. This was to the extent the vast majority troubled to reflect on, or react to, a question then barely on cultural radar screens. I offer—non-authoritatively, of course—my own recollection that heterosexuals spent infinitely less time talking about homosexuals than homosexuals spent talking about themselves. Naturally this state of affairs was bound to end, once the spirit of liberation from bondage, actual or imagined, had spread from blacks to women to Indians to grape-pickers to college students eyeing military call up to, finally, gays, who signaled enthusiastically their readiness for social and legal affirmation.

In truth, the cultural door was wide open to affirmation of just about any kind of sexual expression. If the "hippies" were showing the way, their elders had eyes of their own for the possibilities inherent in a deconstructed moral universe, where everyone got pretty much what he wanted—or tried to. The movies now trafficked in suggestive or flat-out frank depictions of sex; sex manuals offered counsel on style and technique; *Playboy* and *Hustler* offered a great deal more than that—slick-paper passports to private ecstasy. Sex had its political dimension as well: Whatever you were doing, so long as society made a face at it, you were striking a blow for liberty.

No one who gave the matter a moment's thought could have supposed that homosexuality would remain outside the charmed circle of new opportunities. Cultural viewpoints on the matter had been undergoing adjustment virtually since the end of World War II. The famous Kinsey Report of 1948 portrayed homosexuality as far more common than believed, then or since. Dr. Alfred Kinsey, whose taste for the lurid details of other people's sex lives was apparently inexhaustible, asserted that 10 percent of American men were "more or less exclusively homosexual" for at least three years from ages sixteen to fifty-five, whereas 4 percent remained so throughout their lives. Hardly anyone nowadays swallows without a bromide Kinsey's "statistics," gleaned from interviews with sexual blabbermouths, including a disproportionate number of prison inmates. Yet the popularity of his tracts likely eased resistance to the claims that others would make at least partly in his name.

In England, in 1957, a parliamentary report that took a bland view of homosexuality and its consequences resulted in the decriminalization of behavior such as had landed Oscar Wilde in Reading Gaol. With the cultural earthquakes of the 1960s came further invitations to reexamine homosexual experience. In 1974, the American Psychiatric Association removed homosexuality from its list of clinical disorders, on grounds it no longer could responsibly be considered a deviation. Probably no other development came so near to making homosexuality sound—in the ears of its practitioners and advocates, at least—as controversial as a taste for fried chicken or Perry Como. With the APA's action, not all but much of the moral stigma associated with homosexuality simply disappeared.

What did you mean, "illness"? What did you mean, "disorder"? The homosexual had a ready-made reply when challenged to change his ways. Increasingly, it became gospel to homosexuals, as to their "progressive" heterosexual defenders, that sexual orientation was just that—a disposition, a bent, like blonde hair or a taste for iced tea with lemon. There was no helping it, but what of that? Was God's plan for this human or that one to be disrupted by moral outrage or (sometimes worse, in homosexual eyes) religious or psychiatric efforts actually to turn a homosexual into a heterosexual?

I pause again, this time to beg my readers' indulgence. The origins of homosexuality, whether as simple disposition, or as what we often call lifestyle these days, are too vexed a matter for extended discussion in a book about the Episcopal Church. Theories abound. None dominates. I offer in evidence one recent judgment, that of the author of the *Handbook of Child and Adolescent Sexual Problems,* Prof. George Rekers of the University of South Carolina School of Medicine, who "tentatively" concludes that "the main source for gender and sexual behavior is found in social learning and psychological development variables, although we should recognize that there remains the *theoretical possibility* that biological abnormalities *could* contribute a *potential* vulnerability factor in *some* indirect way (italics mine)."

It is hardly the same as saying—in layman's terms, of course— that light comes on when a switch is flipped or teeth rot from too much sugar. Come to think of it, what *are* laymen expected fairly to make of such, shall we say, uncertain evidence as exists concerning the causes of homosexuality? The assertion, by many homosexuals, that gayness is just what one is born with remains an assertion, to be believed by those who want to believe it, to be spurned by those who are having none of it. Whatever might be the actual case, the theological case regarding homosexuality is hard to disentangle from the secular case.

Society at large, in the 1960s, was moving by fits and starts toward greater tolerance of homosexuality—perhaps even to a form of acceptance. What would the churches do? The first thing was, consider their position relative to the culture's fast-evolving position. Accustomed to a leadership role in society, church leaders in all denominations could not but wonder how many Americans would follow their lead in the future if opinion changed so dramatically. It cannot have escaped notice, inside and outside the churches in the late 1960s and early 1970s that the times were turning against the old cultural virtues of obedience, reverence, and restraint. A church unsympathetic to what was going on beyond the stained glass windows might find itself straining harder and harder to be heard.

As for gays and the Episcopal Church . . .

The first detail to note is that gays long have comfortably inhabited the Episcopal/Anglican house of worship: musicians, ordained clergy, lay leaders, worshippers, quite likely out of proportion to the very small percentage of permanent or occasional homosexuals in the general population—an un-Kinseyesque 1.2 percent in the 1990s, by one reckoning. No small reason for this, most would likely agree, is the attraction of gays to a church marked by aesthetic worship, tolerance for contrasting theological and moral perspectives, and a certain reluctance to engage personal questions without some sense of discomfort. Anglicanism's celebrated "breadth"—its habit of making room for all, or nearly all, comers—has made the Episcopal Church a refuge for many who on one ground or another profess disgust with the "moralism" of more demanding or busy-bodyish institutions.

Anglo-Catholicism, which grew out of the mid-nineteenth-century "Oxford" theological movement in England, and which vastly enlarged Anglicanism's appreciation of its apostolic origins, gave to the English and American churches values especially attractive to many gays. Clouds of incense hovered over Anglo-Catholic altars, and richly woven vestments lent theatricality to the ceremony of the Mass (nearly always, in Anglo-Catholic circles, called "the Mass"). From carved choir stalls soared the intricate harmonies of long-bearded composers dead for entire centuries. Less attractive, from an aesthetic standpoint, were the Evangelicals, with their bare-bones liturgical style and strong emphasis on the same "do's and don'ts" that Joseph Fletcher was to pronounce so offensive. The great nineteenth-century English evangelical Charles Kingsley accused the Anglo-Catholics of his day of "a fastidious, maundering die-away effeminacy, which is mistaken for purity and refinement." The whole movement, writes John Shelton Reed, in a study of Kingsley's contemporaries, "was said to produce unladylike women and unmanly men."

The imputation of effeminacy arose logically in the midst of a culture—that of the robust, expansionary Victorian age—that esteemed the virtues of action and order. (The renowned Benjamin Jowett of Oxford University had laid down the non-effeminate creed of the empire-builder: "Never retract, never explain, get it done and let them howl.") Victorian culture prosecuted and jailed Oscar Wilde for sodomy, the same Oscar whose wit and style gave the culture part of its complex and delicious identity. Call it, if you like, a paradox, this cultural willingness to receive the contributions of homosexuals (e.g., *The Importance of Being Earnest, The Picture of Dorian Gray)*, mingled with cultural insistence on the defense of religious and moral norms. In Anglican terms, a good compromise on sexuality was always an unspoken compromise—sensed, never seen.

The Episcopal embrace of gay rights followed, if not accompanied, embrace of the feminist cause, the relationship between the two blocs demonstrating greater strength than the relationship of either to the cause of civil rights. For Americans to embrace the cause of blacks was, if not always easy, entirely logical. The U.S. Constitution commended that cause in so many words. All citizens were due the same rights. Little more, after a certain point, needed saying. It was not so with questions predicated on sex, still less so when some of those questions were seen as dealing not just with sex but also with sexual expression, a fairly different commodity than registering to vote.

The Rev. Malcolm Boyd, hip Episcopal priest, ex-advertising man, best-selling author, and also, behind closed doors, a practicing homosexual, was as well qualified as anyone else to connect the dots. Boyd had marched and demonstrated for civil rights in the South. He inveighed against segregation, war, alienation, and poverty. "As a closeted homosexual," he recalled, "I felt absolutely trapped. I could see no life-giving sexual alternatives. I embraced social activism." With passion, to say the least.

Young Fr. Boyd addressed himself to the plight of poor blacks in inner-city Indianapolis; a co-laborer in the same cause was the future Bishop Paul Moore. At Colorado State University, as a chaplain in the 1950s, Boyd earned the moniker "beatnik priest" for cultural adaptations, e.g., bongo drums, tailored to the presumed needs of the young and alienated. Boyd, the only child of a Wall Street executive who denied his son "masculine love and company," had his first homosexual experience at age ten. He publicly declared himself gay in 1976.

"I was overwhelmed," he would write, a decade and a half later, "by the impossibility of going on forever in a dehumanized mockery of life. It meant subterfuge, guilt, hypocrisy, and the absence of openness. It was even, I profoundly realized, a denial of Jesus Christ." The time had come at last for gays to remove their "masks of repressed anger, self-pity, sexual deceit, hypocrisy, social exploitation, and spiritual arrogance." It was time to walk in the light of freedom. What had come true at last for black Americans—were not gays of all colors entitled to a taste of it?

Nor did Episcopal gays stand nervously by themselves as they made the case for moral parity with non-gays. Plenty of their brothers and sisters who had marched for, or anyway applauded, civil rights, and who rejoiced to see women don priestly vestments, stepped forward to consecrate the cause of gay rights. Who said "rights" were solely political in nature? What of the right to drink the full measure of sexual joy without anxieties of the oh-my-goodness-what-if-someone-finds-out variety? One had to acknowledge the relevance of the question in a society such as America had become by the time Malcolm Boyd jerked open the closet door and peered defiantly out. It was no society of chaperones, onerous repressions, and sanitary goodnight handshakes at a lady's front door, following an evening of lemonade and miniature golf. So much was certain—to the point one hardly could believe one's grandmothers and grandfathers had lived under more than occasionally rigorous codes of moral expectation. The general expectation by the 1970s was that in matters of pleasure and expression Americans would do pretty much what they wanted.

Which was fine, possibly, for those who took their pleasures in the conventional way—man to woman, woman to man. What about the Malcolm Boyds, nevertheless? What about their female equivalents? Was it so large a thing that the objects of their love and interest were physically the same as themselves? People long had said that it mattered, but perhaps such folk were merely bigots, moral matches for the southern sheriffs who had hounded Martin Luther King, Jr. Bishop Paul Moore, ever responsive to the plea of the underdog, would in due course give the point an apocalyptic twist: "The same dangerous mythology that has kept black people in a position of degradation in this country and led to the extermination of the Jews in Nazi Germany surrounds our society's treatment of homosexuality. . . . This mythology is a dangerous mix of sex, violence, and religion." (Moore's testimony took on posthumous poignance with the publication in 2008 of his daughter Honor's account of his life as a bisexual with a male lover. Moore's wife Jenny bore to him nine children—a remarkable total even in that productive era.)

Moore's theme of social and cultural oppression as the lot of gay people is immensely familiar in the 21st century. Gene Robinson, and many more, would embrace and embroider it. The South African archbishop and Nobel laureate Desmond Tutu would announce to the Episcopal Church's 1994 General Convention that "the ordination of homosexuals is an issue of justice."

The debate over homosexuality opened up for feminists a yet larger battlefield. "Heterosexism," wrote Ann E. Gilson, "is the glue which holds sexism in place. It has to do with male control over female sexuality." She was sure that "homophobia," the fear of homosexuals, was but "an attempted reinforcement by the structures of sexism and heterosexism." Strike a blow for the sexual freedom of all and hit male dominance!

Noted Episcopal progressives had no trouble working themselves up over this latest opportunity to rebuke the past. Joseph Fletcher saw "nothing intrinsically good or evil per se in any sexual act." It depended on—what else?—the situation in which it occurred. Then there was John Shelby Spong, the garrulous bishop of Newark, New Jersey, who, in a book titled *Living in Sin: A Bishop Rethinks Human Sexuality*, ambitiously linked women's rights, environmental protection, and world peace as signs of a new "challenge to all previous models of self-understanding, a change in the understanding of the proper balance of power between men and women." Patriarchalism was off, apparently, and with it the subjugating modes of thought and action, including homophobia.

For that matter, on Spong's showing, there was nothing necessarily wrong with divorce, or with conjugal unions conducted outside matrimony. ("Yes, there can be holy sex in the life of a mature single adult.") Homosexuality was merely "an aspect of sexuality," a condition that just *was*, with moral implications no grander, no finer, than those pertaining, as Spong seemed never to tire of saying, to left-handedness. He found that homosexual persons did not choose their own sexual orientation, could not change, and suffered from a form of prejudice that "must take its place alongside witchcraft, slavery, and other ignorant beliefs and oppressive institutions that we have abandoned."

The bishop of Newark had developed a novel conception of morality, one nearer the mark, as he saw it, than the old one, saturated as it was with fantasies of male dominance. "I dare . . . to claim," he said with some sense of satisfaction, "that a new morality is emerging that does manifest the fruits of the Spirit and that is built on the foundation of the mutuality of the sexes." The prophet could be heard, almost, striking his staff on the rock and calling down the Holy Spirit in witness to his insights. He spoke for himself, true, but as he gladly would have claimed if asked, he spoke for numerous others, determined as well as aggrieved.

Was it as simple and straightforward as the bishop of Newark made out? It was to the bishop, certainly, but to many others less so. These (nor was their number insignificant) saw Christian moral belief as less a matter of oppressions instituted at moments of opportunity than a structure revealing the relationship of God Himself to his creation. Was sex merely a vehicle of personal expression, or were there in it elements of profound mystery, embodying the intentions of the Creator regarding his creation? It was useful—rather, it would have been had the restless, angry spirits of the age taken the requisite opportunity—to reflect on such questions.

There certainly were hurdles to overcome before the church aligned itself firmly with those who argued for the moral equivalence of homosexuality and heterosexuality. One very large hurdle was the Bible, which, while it spoke sparingly about homosexuality, said nothing anyone could construe as complimentary of the practice.

Few Episcopalians were likely to be accused of a reverence for the Bible approaching that, say, of the Southern Baptists. Anglicanism's sixteenth-century articles of religion duly asserted that the Bible contained "all things necessary to salvation." Yet this was hardly the same as calling the Bible accurate and authoritative in every jot and title. Most Episcopalians, even conservative ones unsympathetic to the proposed overhaul of Christian morality, were willing to acknowledge that a literalist interpretation of the Bible was no easy thing to bring off, such was the variety in sources, the lavishness of imagery, and the play of human spirit that informed particular passages, as in the Psalms.

A journalist—as I have been for more than four decades— knows how difficult can be the interpretation of even contemporary events and meanings. How much more so the interpretation of words 4,000 and 5,000 years old! And yet the Bible was incontestably the Church's book, its literary charter. It was to be read with patience and respect, not least, perhaps, when its words grated most on the ears and sensibilities. As the seventeenth-century Anglican divine William Sherlock had observed, "To put our own sense on Scripture, without respect to the uses of words, and to the reason and scope of the text" was to "teach it to speak our language." The kindest thing to call such a venture was presumptuous.

As reformists saw it, Scripture afforded large and significant escape clauses, not the least of which was the almost unexceptionable understanding that humans in different ages tend to read words differently, in accordance with events and new knowledge. Nor was Scripture a succession of narratives laid end to end—like bound volumes of the *Wall Street Journal*—for their own sake. "The

Bible," wrote the Episcopal biblical scholar Frederick Borsch in a church-issued study volume, "is not meant to be a written code that kills but a vehicle of the Spirit that gives life." Where the spirit was moving, the wise would certainly follow, irrespective of what their predecessors might have said and done. In the jargon of modernity, human understanding of God's purpose was "a work in progress."

Which brings us to Scripture's viewpoint concerning homosexuality. Even if there was not a great deal in them to chew on, the relevant passages had a pronounced flavor. There was the famous account in Genesis of the angels who visited Lot in the city of Sodom, where they appear (v. 5) to have become the object of carnal interest on the part of the local men, "both young and old." In Judges 19, a Levite had a similar encounter in Gibeah. The Levitical law (Lev. 18:22 and 20:13) condemned in almost the same breath homosexual relations and bestiality. As for the New Testament, St. Paul, in 1 Cor. 6:9-10, had cited "homosexuals" (re-translated male prostitutes and sodomites in the New Revised Standard Version) among the unexalted company (adulterers, thieves, drunkards, etc.) whose behavior would exclude them from the kingdom of God. Likewise, in Romans 1:21-27, Paul had reckoned among the wicked both men and women who "exchanged natural relations for unnatural."

It was certainly bleak fare from the viewpoint of homosexuals seeking acceptance, which is no doubt why it stuck so fast in their craw. Where was the affirmation Scripture was expected to provide the lonely and downtrodden—the clap on the back, the warm welcome? Why so dry and wizened a way of looking at a minority whose cause the secular society was beginning to take up with some zeal? This really wouldn't do, not if the Episcopal Church was to face a revolutionary age in a spirit of receptiveness rather than adamant opposition.

What churches came to realize by the 1970s was that a large, dissatisfied corps of Christians and non-Christians saw them as blocking the path to the affirmation that homosexuals sought— the latest minority to claim rights they viewed as due them. Surely no God worth His incense would read out of His kingdom human beings whose tastes might differ from other people's but who were likely, at bottom, as worthy as anyone else! Weren't there other ways to read the biblical strictures, or to put them in perspective?

No small number of hands shot up in response to the invitation. The Rev. Norman Pittenger, who had trained many a future Episcopal priest at the General Theological Seminary in New York City, and who had helped shape a widely used Episcopal "teaching series" in the 1950s, found the task of revision perfectly agreeable, inasmuch as he himself was gay. He dismissed St. Paul's pronouncements as "a reflection of his Jewish background, in which homosexuality was taken to be tied in with the human tendency to idolatry." Additionally, according to Pittenger, Paul was reacting to the general licentiousness of the age (an interesting claim for Pittenger to address to denizens of the *Playboy*-hippie-New Morality world!).

It was a mere sample, albeit a pithy one, of the arguments reformers would use to redirect the church's thinking on homosexuality, and on the place of homosexuals and lesbians in church affairs. What St. Paul said in the first century A.D. (or "C.E.," for "Common Era," as religious pluralists had begun deferentially dating New Testament time) cried out, it seemed, for constructive reinterpretation in the twentieth century. Had not the Episcopal Church already sifted Paul's remarks about women ("Wives, be subject to your husbands," "the head of a woman is her husband," etc.) for discardable dross in order that women might safely be ordained as priests? From the lectionary of the 1979 prayer book, such embarrassing passages had been drained, then dropped down the Orwellian memory hole.

Other scholars and commentators weighed in to the same effect. The Genesis narrative was slippery, with the Sodomites' offense looking more like an affront to hospitality than anything else. As for the sexual practices that offended Paul, wasn't the Apostle talking about exploitative sex with underlings—slaves, boys, and the like? In which case the right way to see Paul was as a man with important things to say to his own time—things, nevertheless, that in particular cases had lost relevance over the centuries.

A favorite shibboleth of many who support the homosexual agenda is the insufficiency of biblical witness in moral matters due to supposed biblical sanction for slavery. Yet another favorite gambit: the general irrelevance or cruelty of Levitical law, e.g., "A man or a woman who is a medium or a wizard shall be put to death" (Lev. 20:27). *Surely* no modern person supports burning witches! Besides all this, Jesus never mentioned homosexuality. Never. Having launched on the enterprise of biblical overhaul, one discovers how many surprising, and tantalizing, possibilities come to mind.

The task of biblical reinterpretation had, of course, Pandoran qualities. What else besides a new view of homosexuality would fly out of the box, its lid having been pried open? If the Bible had got it wrong about homosexuality (or if we ourselves had got it wrong on account of the Bible's getting it wrong), what else in the great Book required rethinking and reworking? Perhaps, as the atheists suggested, the whole thing was shot through with distortions and myths. A document whose authority underwent continual challenge could end with hardly any authority that the intelligent were bound to recognize. When reading the Bible, maybe it was best . . . One moment here: George and Ira Gershwin's "Sportin' Life," in *Porgy and Bess,* comes to mind, with his choice words of counsel: "Oh, I takes dat gospel whenever it's pos'ble/But wid a grain o' salt."

"Wid" a grain of salt, indeed, to avoid confusion of past purposes with present ones. You never could tell. You could suspect, nonetheless. The reinterpretive effort went remorselessly forward. John Boswell, a gay historian at Yale University, in a widely reviewed and widely cited book, *Christianity, Social Tolerance, and Homosexuality,* suggested that much of what we knew about premodern morality was wrong or misleading. The early Christians, said Boswell, were not given to fretting over homosexuality, on which the New Testament took "no demonstrable position." Nor had the early middle ages found much to say about the matter. Only in the high middle ages did approval dissolve, for reasons Boswell found it "not possible to analyze." (The locution was comparable to others on which he leaned constantly: "It is possible"; "It seems at least fair to infer"; "the evidence suggests"; "there is no room to believe" etc., etc.). Boswell died of AIDS before nailing down his case with the certainty it might have been thought to require.

Perhaps no decisive evidence on this score was essential. Perhaps in the age of civil rights and feminism and moral disarray, to raise the specter of doubt was enough. What certainly was true— never mind the nocturnal intentions of the men of Sodom—was that the moral revolution of the 1960s had opened to homosexuals opportunities they meant firmly to appropriate in all contexts of life, religious as well as secular. They had achieved victimhood, than which, in the late twentieth century there was, ironically enough, no loftier status. Blacks had been victims. Women— according to powerful elements of the culture, male and female alike—had been victims. Society had embraced their respective grievances and set out on the path of atonement. Now it was gays who clamored for attention. It was impossible to pass by on the other side of the road while they lay battered and pleading. Something had to be done, reasoned the Episcopal Church, among other prestigious organizations, both secular and religious.

The irony was that, in seeming to refute St. Paul and deconstruct the Sodom account, the new reformers believed themselves to have done all that theology required. It was a facile notion. It was even more than that: It was dangerous. St. Paul had used a word of which too little notice perhaps had been taken. The word was "natural." Many (Rom.1:27) had exchanged "natural relations for unnatural." What was that about? There was a decided implication here that proponents of gay rights were unwilling to explore in depth, namely, that certain modes of life were congruent with divine purpose, whereas other modes were not. Was there indeed a nature to which created beings were expected to conform themselves and their actions?

Such a question seemed worth at least a few moments' notice—which was more moments than normal in discussions of gay rights. The first datum available for notice was the general public's general failure to buy into this newest civil rights cause. The majority of Americans seemed not to like what they were hearing about the need for incorporation of homosexuality into the country's daily pastimes and, as we were coming to say, "lifestyles." It was one thing, seemingly, to acknowledge that gays were there—wherever "there" was—and to accept the need to deal with them decently and honorably, especially when AIDS began felling homosexuals right and left. It was quite another matter to accept that homosexuality and heterosexuality were merely flip sides of the same human craving for emotional and physical fulfillment. As for AIDS, was it not known to be a consequence of homosexual relations, among other things?

The public at large seemed to sense something that their theological teachers, many of them, failed to sense. Might that thing be the impropriety of using the body for ends not suggested by the Creator's blueprint?

Maybe no civil rights question was after all at stake. Maybe the basic question was congruency with the divine will and purpose. Look at men. Look at women. See the ways they functioned together. God had made things one way. He had not made them another. Opinion polls to the present day show majority opposition—though less of it than ten or twenty years ago—to proposals for the legalization of same-sex marriage. The generality of Americans simply don't buy into the cultural contentions of the gay rights movement, though you'd be hard-pressed sometimes to know it from reading *The New York Times* or listening to Rosie O'Donnell.

It was not only to Romans that one could trace the sense of something terribly amiss in the couplings of men with men, women with women. Whatever the value of John Boswell's investigations, the greatest minds of their respective times had added assent to the strong inferences of Scripture as to the undesirability, if not also the physical impracticality, of same-sex relationships.

Augustine, in the *Confessions*, deplored "those offenses which be contrary to nature." Thus also Aquinas in the *Summa Theologica* (*II II. Q.* 154. 12): "Just as the ordering of right reason proceeds from man, so the order of nature is from God Himself: wherefore in sins contrary to nature, whereby the very order of nature is violated, an injury is done to God, the Author of nature."

Different centuries, same argument. Heterosexual relations reflected and furthered the grand design of the Creator; it was same-sex relationships that affronted the design. The Book of Common Prayer, as we have noted, spoke to the matter.

The matter was not merely physical; it was ontological. Maleness was the male condition. So with females and femaleness. Was all this Thomist ordering-of-nature stuff just philosophical folderol, valueless for the most part to real people? A fundamental point was the ease with which gay rights advocates turned the argument: "God made me gay" became increasingly the contention, advanced with the certainty of a poker player calling the pot while eying appreciatively his own straight flush. The hearer was supposed to reciprocate: "Well, yes, of course, if that's who you are . . . "

On the other hand, if the hearer had heard, and if he believed, that God made man and woman for the purposes of mutual fulfillment and procreation, he was apt to reply: "Well, you see, we can't have gay 'marriage' because it wouldn't work, marriage according to the holy ordinances of God meaning union between a man and a woman." The hearer might add that it would be hardly right to have in charge of congregations and dioceses gay priests whose lives exemplified a doctrine of marriage other than the one the church affirmed.

The obvious "out" here is to change the doctrine. On which enterprise the Episcopal Church—amid considerable dissent, it needs emphasizing—seems to have launched itself. The moral tradition of the Christian faith points to a different outcome than that for which the Episcopal Church labors.

It may be too late to ask what the Episcopal Church should do about the question of same-sex relationships. The church is far along the admittedly rock-strewn road leading to full ratification of those relationships. Not yet have Episcopalians given explicit approval to the ordination of practicing gay men, and to marriage rites for gay couples. Yet the consecration of Gene Robinson, and the enthusiasm with which that consecration still meets in exalted church circles, shows how far a once-inconceivable journey has progressed.

The church's presiding bishop, Katharine Jefferts Schori, proudly affirms the apparent Episcopal commitment to gay rights. Likewise, she affirms Gene Robinson's right to preside over the Episcopal Diocese of New Hampshire. If a man living amorously with a man qualifies as a bishop of the church, what bars a similarly circumstanced man or woman from elevation to any church office whatever? What, by that same token, could prevent the church from devising rites for same-sex couples wishing it to bless and consecrate and generally affirm the truth and validity of their relationship? If it comes to that, I can think of nothing, now, that bars the way. An Episcopal prayer book rite for gay unions, whether or not civil law allows for such, seems to me an eventual certainty, sooner rather than later.

The question I raise is not so much what policies the church might now adopt as it is what might have come of thinking through *as a church*—rather than as a kind of social service community with a taste for ecclesiastical language—the question of gay relationships.

Had the Episcopal Church cared actually to reflect on the gay rights question, it might have avoided wounding itself in noisy and spectacular fashion, on television and in the newspapers. Whereas outraged "conservatives" (so to style them) had stayed on in the church through prayer-book revision and women's ordination, many saw gay rights as the proverbial final straw—the bridge too far. Over it they could not and would not walk.

And so it came to pass, a half-millennium after Anglicanism's debut in North America, that a welter of Anglican affiliates in Virginia and Florida and Pennsylvania and California and elsewhere—Anglican but self-connected to jurisdictions in Kenya or Nigeria or Singapore or Chile—was walking and worshiping in place of the old church with the Gothic archways and sonorous language. Local churches wrenched themselves away from the larger church, sometimes taking along their property, sometimes walking away from everything in order to begin anew. Episcopal priests, giving vent at last to long-suppressed doubts about their leadership, accused fellow Episcopal priests and Episcopal bishops, as well, of abandoning the Christian faith. The name of the Episcopal Church became in many places, for the very first time, a stigma rather than an attraction, an embarrassment instead of a badge—with what consequences for Christian evangelism almost anyone can imagine.

What if, instead, when the Episcopal Church first heard the cultural clamor for gay rights, it had put to itself, prayerfully and thoughtfully, just three questions? There might have been more worth consideration. These are three that occur to me:

Question 1. The purpose of sex is *what* exactly? And who decides?

I can imagine, fifty or sixty years ago, such a question being described as inappropriate, if not in disgusting taste. In one of the least prim, most relaxed epochs on record (consider merely what you saw and heard at the last movie you went to) one can't imagine embarrassing Mrs. Grundy with sex talk or "bad" language. Such being so, where are the theologians now? More to the point, where were they when gay rights talk first fell on Episcopal ears?

It was not that theologians refused to talk. Many, like Spong, refused to *quit* talking. It was that they declined much of the time to talk in theological terms—that is, in terms of the purposes of Almighty God, who, unless he had been deceiving His followers for a remarkably long time, formed this earth and everything in it, including men and women, for purposes that were His own, hence subject only to His own will, not that of these willful creatures.

Now if a church is going to reinvent its sexual theology, one might suppose it means to talk thoughtfully of how better, and more clearly, to understand the purposes that Almighty God means sex to serve. And how do we do that? First—wouldn't you think?—by meditating long on existing beliefs on this score and asking whether or not some deeper purpose that up to now had escaped the church was to be served by the legitimizing of same-sex relationships.

Always the church had been of one mind on marriage and sex, discounting, for the most part, twentieth-century speculations generated in the Yale history department and like venues. Whatever in human affairs might at any time have gone amiss with the practice of marriage, still the doctrine, the teaching, reflected centuries of prayerful Christian reflection. The purely physical specifications fit no combination but that of man and woman. None but a man and a woman could create life. A man and a man—never; a woman and a woman—the same. This was not even to mention the mutual support and sustenance to be had through the merger of the two sensibilities, male and female, neither complete, neither full, lacking this attribute or that one. An advocate of homosexual rights could object that, well, when it came to mutual support, anyone could want and need that. But did simple yearning render homosexuality a morally neutral aspect of the divine scheme?

If it did, few—very few—ever had thought so. If so few indeed had thought so, perhaps it was up to the proponents of change to explain why the point had been missed for so long. In other words, where was the evidence for calls to align homosexual and heterosexual practice as mere evidences of different strokes sought by different folks? Who said so? John Spong said so. But listen to him (as in *Living in Sin*): "Personhood emerges not out of an imposed sexual role but out of the human ability to hear, feel, think, and relate. None of these abilities requires sex organs of any shape or description. . . . There is nothing unnatural about any shared love, even between two of the same gender, if that experience calls both partners into a fuller state of being." Er, says who? Says Bishop Spong—without reference, be it noted, to Christian reflection on the matter. This is theology by assertion: I say so, therefore—

There is more than this to the matter. Why *not* a rousing debate on sexuality? Is there a theory, a premise, a custom, a settled piece of wisdom we shrink from debating, rousingly or otherwise? A church encountering such a debate and proposing to enter it is obliged—wouldn't one think?—to keep theological assumption and argument at the center of things, in order to stand discreetly apart from the program and purposes of the Democratic or Republican parties, or the Harvard political science faculty, or the newest Washington, D.C., think tank, all enterprises well-equipped to get along without ecclesiastical counsel. There was of course no reason for a Christian church *not* to hear the viewpoints of the secular society. Yet showcasing those viewpoints could mean treating the Creator as just one more team member, albeit an experienced one, on a large and crowded playing field.

About the only thing Episcopal advocates of gay rights have managed to advance from a theological or quasi-theological perspective is the notion that God bids the "inclusion" of all people in the divine design. Yes, but did inclusion in that design mean, as gay rights proponents seemed to suggest, acceptance on the mere basis of membership in a certain group? That was certainly the civil rights-entitlement approach; yet what applicability had that approach to the matter of those terms on which individual sinners ultimately stand before the throne of God—as advertised in Scripture?

We have heard of collective guilt heretofore. What inclusionists argue for is collective innocence: group membership, identity, as the grounds for incorporation into the community of the forgiven. (In a way, what a very Episcopal attitude, one that plays off old-time Episcopal satisfaction with membership in such a country-clubbish body of Christian people.)

The inclusionist position skirts, by generally ignoring, the whole question of personal sin and accountability for same, a question that many modern Christians, far from all of them Episcopalians, find disagreeable and embarrassing. Inclusionism, perhaps inadvertently, reduces sex to a behavioral proposition: Am I loving? Am I responsible? Do I affirm and support my partner? And if I am these things, and do these things, does that not clinch the deal? (Bishop Gene Robinson's apologists point to the committed love that Robinson and his male partner supposedly show for each other, as if no more about their relationship required saying, not even that Robinson's deliberate embrace of the relationship wrecked a heterosexual marriage that had produced two daughters.)

The purpose of sex is . . . what exactly? Far be it from twenty-first-century Episcopalians to say in an overtly theological way.

Question 2. If we actually were to have a theological discussion of sex, how much sense would it make to sweep off the table as irrelevant, misguided, homophobic—whatever the opprobrious term of the moment—the moral teaching of two thousand years? How does one judge a new teaching but by the old, held up to the light for comparison?

A glorious modern (i.e., post-Enlightenment) delusion is that of knowing so much about psychology, biology, physics, chemistry, geology, and engineering that what relatively little our forebears knew seems of marginal utility. The whole thrust of modern culture is to denigrate ancient wisdom as perhaps no wisdom at all. Oh, the best, maybe, that one might have hoped for under the straitened circumstances of ye olden times— yet still, in the light of all we now know!) sadly deficient and uninformative.

Not the least shame here is sending away from the table the likes of Augustine and Aquinas, to say nothing of Paul, who might welcome a chance to explain himself as other than a misogynistic homophobe ("a self-loathing homosexual," as Bishop Spong once charmingly described him).

Still another advantage of putting past and present together at the table is caution born of humility. Many modern Episcopalians, it regularly seems to me, would benefit from immersion in the thought of a great secular Anglican, Edmund Burke, whose classic work *Reflections on the Revolution in France* is a sort of handbook of prudence in the context of accelerated emotion. "A spirit of innovation is generally the result of a selfish temper and confined views," wrote Burke to his countrymen and the world. "People will not look forward to posterity, who never look backwards to their ancestors." Again: "It is a presumption in favor of any settled scheme of government against any untried project [the exaltation of gay rights?], that a nation [or a church a civilization?] has long existed and flourished under it."

If the foregoing was the counsel of statecraft, how could that exclude it from consideration by church executives, bishops, and so on, who behave routinely as political practitioners, constantly giving advice on political issues, working to shape large cultural issues to their own liking? "[I]t is with infinite caution," wrote Burke, "that any ought to venture upon pulling down an edifice which has answered in any tolerable degree for ages the common purpose of society, or on building it up again, without having models and patterns of approved utility before his eyes." Models, say, from an old book once foundational to the life and worship of the church?

Question 3. The value of railing at those who call merely for prudent, theologically centered discussion of moral matters . . . that value is *what*, exactly?

A really startling feature of gay-rights rhetoric in our time is its accusatory tone. We hear in its language the voice not of the humble Christian teacher seeking to reconcile worldly realities with the will of God; we hear, instead, the voice of the prosecuting attorney. Down comes the fist on the table. I'm right! You're wrong! The voice is one we recognize well enough from Christian history, the be-damned-to-you voice of the suddenly inspired: Cromwell; Savonarola; John Brown of Kansas; the yahoos, may I add, from elsewhere in Kansas, members of a Baptist church who sometimes troop around the country, forcing strident, anti-gay rhetoric on people with no wish to hear it. It all makes for a cacophony of voices—the more grating, like a cell phone twittering away during a violin sonata, when the topic is profoundly serious, such as what to make of sex.

The moral certainty of the Episcopal Church's gay rights proponents has served, both deliberately and accidentally, a variety of purposes, including the election of at least one gay bishop and presumably the election of more, all in good time. Whether making the church inhospitable to Episcopalians of traditional viewpoint—a major upshot of the Robinson consecration—was accidental or intentional, I could not presume to say. I might speculate that both factors—accident and intention—played their parts.

To some in the church, the morally conservative are a ghastly encumbrance, a barrier to progress. "Let 'em go" is not the same as "Make 'em go," but it seems fair to guess that when the Episcopal

Church shatters at last into a roomful of constituent parts, and gay rights is accounted by all parties a major cause of the destruction, not a few proponents of the new moral order will laugh aloud in joy and relief, and rub their hands in satisfaction for the loss of their adversaries.

How a traditionalist exodus from the church could further the church's mission of Gospel presentation—perhaps an answer will yet suggest itself. None has revealed itself so far.

TEN 〰
Lighten Our Darkness

S0 WHERE ARE WE? Comes time to bring these varied strands of narrative together—to stack them alongside each other in some coherent context. The doings of a single church, or a collection of churches, have no greater relevance than those of—well, professional baseball, or the New York Philharmonic, or Scottish Rite Masonry. No greater relevance, that is, unless a church happens to stand in some special relationship to Almighty God, and its manner of thinking and acting incorporates urgent glimpses of realities outside the line of normal vision. In which case, yes—the doings of a church matter vitally, as affairs of life and of death.

The mellow traditionalism that defined the old Episcopal Church—respectful of the less-than-dewy-fresh, skeptical of the abrasively, aggressively radical—is out the door and down the street. "And good riddance!" exclaim many of those who chased it from the premises, arguing that a church of brokers and bankers, a church placid, tame, complacent, set in its ways—a church of Episcopal traits and dimensions, in fine—cannot be such a church as the twenty-first century needs and requires.

Well? Can it be?

That might depend on what a church is supposed to do: respond to present-day pressures in the manner of a policy organization, or guard with zeal—for the sake of proclaiming with credibility—those foundational "truths" said to proceed from God and nowhere else. Among them: human sinfulness, with pride at its shriveled root; repentance as the price of forgiveness, through God's only Son, who died for the world's sins; love of God and of one's neighbor as the essential human pursuit; the Scriptures as the faithful record of God's works and will in the world; the devil as mortal enemy of man. And so forth, the creeds summing it all up with magnificent economy. If a church is charged, by its Lord, with the duty of keeping all such considerations together for the purposes of ministry and salvation, it may be that a church of old-time Episcopal traits and dimensions is not so bad a thing after all.

Whatever its human limitations, including its commitment (or, to put it another way, the commitment of its members) to the rights and privileges of affluence, the old Episcopal Church helped underwrite religious stability and tamp down revolutionary impulses and inclinations. As did—it surely goes without saying—the other, now-vexed outposts of the American Christian mainline. I mean to praise, not damn. I need to make that clear in view of the modern expectation that the more restlessness you come across inside a moss-encrusted institution of any kind, the better it is for all concerned. Not always. Not by any means. A volatile, unstable faith, subject to constant change, is more bulletin board than faith, a series of exchanges on matters and topics unconnected to each other, or to any overarching structure of belief and purpose. Who needs faithless faith, except as diversion, or, better still, as cover and excuse for social activism, group empowerment, and the like? Once we begin, in the modern manner, to equate religion with politics and "improvement," of a mainly secular sort, we put religion on a new plane.

The old Episcopal Church of the muttered truths and faithfully enacted rituals had, like every other human institution, clear imperfections in the sight of God. It had moments of sublimity as well. It further enjoyed rewards of a special kind for the steady defense of truths more durable than those often seen chasing their tails around and around the Internet. Likewise the Methodists, the Presbyterians, and so on—who deserve respect for their historic confidence in the integrity of the revelation entrusted to them. What happened to the Episcopalians happened, in some measure, to all. Truth, theological truth, became a more shadowy commodity than before.

In the Episcopal Church of the twenty-first century, truth is a moving target, dynamic, rarely at rest. Whereas, for instance, heterosexual monogamy was the foundational truth the Church historically received with respect to biological yearnings, truth for many modern Episcopalians is that God accepts a "loving" and "committed" relationship of nearly any kind. The point, for Episcopalians given to this second mode of understanding, is never to shut down the possibility of God's showing us something *fresh*— like a breathless young TV correspondent on Action Central News; like a bleary blogger at Starbucks.

"Truth has many facets to it, as opposed to the view that there is one truth," a former presiding bishop, Frank Griswold, has said.

In fact, one truth generally looks, to many Episcopalians, greener than all the rest: the truth that Episcopalians, having had things too good for too long, need comprehensively to privilege the un- or under-privileged minorities: women, homosexuals, outsiders of every kind and description. No "male, patriarchal Anglo-Saxon" vision binds and blinds Episcopalians any more. "Diversity" is our calling card, all to be celebrated and affirmed. Not just as neighbors either, but as moral beings, the old unitary view of morality having lost preeminence as new ways of expressing love to the loved come into view. Hence the need for tolerance, a trait long identified with easygoing, non-censorious Episcopalianism, broadened now to downplay distinctions of practically every sort, except perhaps on special occasions.

I was oddly charmed to read recently *The New York Times*'s account of a conversation with a woman affirming the equivalence of all views on the "holidays," our country's new term for the whole month of December. This woman likened the "holiday" experience to a sociological block party, with everyone encouraged to bring his favorite dish. "I think we should all celebrate everything," she said. "We should have Christmas, we should have Hanukkah, and whatever people have. I think we should all learn to respect each other. Everyone should have the right to be who they are. That's what the country is all about." I do not believe she was Episcopalian. She might well have been, though.

The modern Episcopal love affair with tolerance and diversity and contrasting views of truth has had very specific effects on the church's ability to function as a church—an institution, it sometimes seems, more loosely wedded to the passing earthly show than to the Kingdom of Heaven.

The mood of the Episcopal Church, as it wended from the 1960s into the 1970s, then into the 1980s and 1990s, was one of increasing concern for those markers and measures the secular world set out. The secular world spoke to the dilemma of women as women themselves portrayed it, "sexism" barring the way to fulfillment and achievement. Then the world spoke, a little more haltingly but with growing exasperation, about embedded attitudes toward homosexuals, about laws and customs that denied them the social affirmation for which they supposedly yearned. In both cases, Episcopalians moved, as a church, to the front lines, offering all the help at their disposal to the putative victims, whose story became *their* story.

The standards of the world had become, in considerable measure, the standards of the Episcopal Church. There once had been some notion that this was getting the matter backwards. Was it not the church's role to acclimate the world outside the church to the expectations of the risen Lord? Did not those expectations trump the earnest grunts and groans of the secular world? Why now, if so, the adaptation of those expectations to those of the world, and on what conceivable grounds?

Episcopalians were supposed to know better than blindly to follow the culture of the world—at least, by their own self-measure they were supposed to. There was a careful Anglican standard for judging truth. It was three-fold and more than a little daunting when taken with utmost seriousness. I have mentioned the matter before. Allow me to lift the covering slightly higher.

First, under the Anglican theory, the Scriptures were taken as representing divine authority: nothing there but the will of God. Whatever an Anglican needed for salvation, there he found it, as the Sixth Article of Religion declared. The church itself was servant to and keeper of the Word. It lacked power, so the Twentieth Article of Religion said, "to ordain any thing that is contrary to God's Word written." Nothing else could the church force "to be believed for necessity of Salvation" other than what Scripture taught.

The Anglican resort to Scripture was neatly hedged for safety's sake. How one read Scripture was in part a function of how the Church had read and reflected upon it—the Church, that great collectivity of Christians stretching from Rome to London to Moscow to San Francisco to Rio de Janeiro, around the world and back again. The attenuated sense in which modern people use the term "tradition" recalls the full sense: wisdom and knowledge studied, honed, refined, passed from one generation to the next, and to the next, as embodying the truth, as incarnating reality.

Whatever the church had taught with undiminished commitment and enthusiasm, that teaching gained in authenticity as time went by. We had not outgrown it. We had grown into it. It was part of us, for which there might well be holy reasons.

The last of the three great norms for understanding truth was the activity of the mind, the mind given by God, known as reason. Reason constituted the third leg of that which Anglicans called their three-legged stool for the ratification or rejection of ideas about God and the Kingdom. Reason sorted out and evaluated whatever material was before it, taking into full account the witness of Scripture and tradition. As Archbishop Michael Ramsey would appraise the matter: "Reason increases and enlarges human understanding of divine revelation through its own workings, so long as reason is used in humble dependence upon the God who gave it."

The Anglican approach was balanced, as one might expect of a faith balanced (once again, as an ideal) between Protestantism and Catholicism, between fanaticism and apathy, between varied styles of ceremonial and practice and custom.

I would myself guess that in a grossly unbalanced age—our own age, let us say—a religion of balance is an early candidate for disruption, no church walls being high or thick enough to keep out the spirit of that age. The question would be, of course, once the spirit got inside, how you would treat it—whether with resistance, skepticism, or joyous embrace.

When the spirit of the twentieth century—the *zeitgeist*—barged into the Episcopal Church, muddying the carpets and knocking over delicate vases full of hibiscus, the church, unaccountably to many, welcomed it to the front pew. Many Episcopalians were happy to have such a visitor. They liked its brash, uninhibited style, to which, increasingly, they adjusted their own style and standards. These wanted a church in tune with all that was going on outside the church—the dissonance, the flash and vulgarity, the noise and the sheer excitement.

That the church, on the basis of its intimacy with the only begotten Son of God, might already have unique gifts to impart was a notion that entered the heads of too few Episcopal bishops and theologians. In no time, progressive Episcopalians began to speak of visits from another spirit—the Holy Spirit, the one identified by Paul (*1 Cor. 2:11*) as revealing the thoughts of God. The attribution to the Holy Spirit of a will to overthrow old standards, old arrangements, is one of the persistent themes in recent Episcopal history. Not long after the General Convention of 2006, an Episcopal publication ran a letter that epitomized that theme. "If we accept the idea that Jesus reflects the will and nature of our Creator," said the letter-writer, a priest, "then it appears that God isn't male-biased. The Holy Spirit, whose guidance we always seek when we consider making changes in the Church, must be leading us toward egalitarianism and away from autocracy and a hierarchical form of polity."

How was that again? The Spirit was saying . . . *what*? And how were others to know it was truly the Spirit talking and not just some angry inner voice? Where was the proof? As to women's ordination, the issue with which the letter-writer was immediately concerned, why had no promptings of the Holy Spirit reached the Roman Catholics and the Orthodox, who continue to understand the all-male priesthood as God's will for the Church? Was it that the Spirit particularly liked Episcopalians? How was one to know? Where was the proof? None has ever been forthcoming.

What happens, I have observed, is that when a sufficient number of prestigious Episcopalians, such as bishops, claims to hear the Spirit's voice, that settles matters. Those to whom the Spirit evidently has nothing to say become obligated—in the words of a noted Episcopalian, Robert E. Lee, at Appomattox Courthouse—to "yield to overwhelming numbers and resources." Not that mere head-counting discloses divine will. (Hitler got the votes of most Germans, after all.) What it does do is provide cultural and political momentum. In the intensely political atmosphere of the present, a head count is something most Americans recognize as an instrument of, at the very least, social peace.

Further, by the time of the eruptions of the 1960s and 1970s, a kind of auxiliary test was providing color snapshots of the Spirit. The testing device was experience, of the human variety. Episcopal leaders became fond of urging the allegedly oppressed to "tell their stories," as information essential to the raising of general consciousness.

There would seem to be value in such a measuring stick, if to *do* is better than to *imagine.* Yet how does anyone really know, individually or collectively, what meaning is assignable to experience, singular or plural? A church committed to the objective character of truth, when it let down its buckets into the well of pure experience, was committing itself to a highly subjective, highly intimate method of sensing God's will, "sensing" more than "apprehending"—the heart over the head—in good late twentieth-century fashion. The personal, it seemed, could now in some sense trump the collective, the accumulated, the amassed wisdom of many generations and centuries. To say nothing of its effect on the authority stemming (one's forebears had believed) from the word of God as written down and transmitted in Scripture. Whatever else one might say of the new test, experience, it was at least democratic. Anyone with a voice or, especially, a grievance, could play.

And so, with a minimum of theological debate, women's ordination came to the Episcopal Church. Some of the massive liturgical transformations of the 1970s had scholarship behind them, though not scholarship of an undisputed kind (e.g., why did Baptism now constitute full initiation into the Church, whereas Confirmation by the bishop had previously been deemed essential?). Sin, that old-time symbol of the conflict between God and Satan, took on new configurations. The advancement of earthly goals like "peace" and "justice" took precedence over goals felt to inhibit personal expression. Brisker modes of worship took hold, compatible with the brisker pace of the secular world. Within the church, divorce moved from scandal to excusable interruption—to match events outside the church. The spirit—of the age, that is—had helped to engineer these changes and transitions. A precedent was set. At those intersections where the ways of the church contradicted and blocked the ways of the culture, the culture had prevailed. It could prevail again.

It did, when the issue moved from sex (women's ordination) to sexuality (same-sex relationships). Here, as we have seen, Scripture and tradition had been unsparing in their negativism toward homosexuality. Two legs of the three-legged stool contradicted the desire of many within the church to execute an about-face on homosexuality. It was going to be necessary once more to enlist the Spirit, still resting up from persuading the Episcopal General Convention that it desired the ordination of women.

The equality of all Christians was again the theme. All Christians were the same. To deprive one set was to break the bonds of unity and charity, and to buy into old myths that modern people no longer believed in concerning homosexuals, who, as experience showed, were often solid, producing members of the community, not to mention valued toilers in the Lord's vineyard. It turned out that, just as women of the church had suffered from patriarchalism, gays and lesbians had received unwarranted chastisement as a result of "homophobia"—literally, fear of homosexuals, but reinterpreted in the twentieth century as actual, visceral, hatred of them, a sick sentiment I have never witnessed in actual performance.

At last the job was, if not completed, then commenced in earnest, with the consecration of a practicing homosexual as bishop of the church and, finally, the crack and crunch of a church breaking apart on the shoals. Again the argument had turned on cultural rather than theological claims: homosexuals as citizens badly abused and unfairly put upon by society, rather than (as Scripture had more than implied and the church had affirmed in its moral teachings and marriage canons) practitioners of a sexual style at odds with the divine scheme for the living of life.

That was possibly an interesting point, yet one that took no notice of the Western world's new creed—liberation, empowerment, diversity, equality, and inclusiveness. A church standing in the way of these ideals was not a church such as the secular culture cared to commend to anyone but its members, and maybe not to them, either.

Another thing was curious—and curiously disturbing—about the new order in the church. In theory, a new order of tolerance and inclusion tolerates and includes all "truths," according old truths as much scope as the new ones claimed for themselves when they rode into view. Matters have not, to say the least, turned out this way. The establishment, having won (with, no doubt, the Spirit's invaluable assistance), decided to consolidate its varied victories by instructing the defeated, in essence, to stuff it.

The prayer book of 1979 was shoved down the throats of dioceses and parishes that saw, not without reason, much good in the one that was being cast out. Bishops and liturgiologists grounded their response in the need for "common" prayer. It was a strange contention, inasmuch as the new book hardly represented "common" prayer, with its "modern" language (Rite II) versions of the Eucharist, Morning Prayer, Evening Prayer, and Burial, and its traditional, if pared down, (Rite I) versions.

Devotees of the 1928 book and its majestic cadences, its profound theology, wished to know how the church's historic liturgy had suddenly become so objectionable that bishops ordained under it were actually forbidding its use (except perhaps at early Sunday morning services, where it was seen as an ancient rite for the chronologically ancient, souls too stiff or too unimaginative to hear and heed the Spirit's promptings). There is no way to quantify the losses of members, and even whole congregations, in consequence of prayer book revision—or, rather, this particular style of revision. The numbers were considerable all the same, not least, in my own judgment, on account of the church's disregard of "diversity" where, so the church believed, no reasonable church could countenance diversity.

A church vexed with such divisions might have sought delay in answering "the spirit's" next call, which was to rout sexism from the church. Not so. The vote to allow women's ordination preceded by three years the final ratification of the new prayer book, which itself preceded by only three years the final ratification of a new hymnal. For a church supposedly set in its ways, the Episcopal Church showed deep commitment to deliberate speed, majestic instancy.

The vote to ordain women was for many catholic-minded Episcopalians the straw that broke the camel's back. Out they went to found "continuing" churches, bodies likely more successful at providing refuge for the ecclesiastically afflicted than at winning the world for Christ. Yet, collectively, the continuing churches were a reproach to the church from which they had detached themselves, one palpably more concerned about being in step with the surrounding secular culture than with the vaster community of Christians who had for centuries affirmed another way—and who were, after all, dead.

Nor, as it came to pass, was the church going to tolerate what might be called alternative, if culturally discredited, viewpoints on the matter—even when the viewpoint was that on which the church had insisted prior to 1976. The three dioceses—Fort Worth, Texas; San Joaquin, California; Quincy, Illinois—that held out against the new order, long after the cave-in of other catholic dioceses, found that freedom of choice was not a luxury to be accorded "conservatives." Feminists of the more rambunctious type got the General Convention to order the hold-out dioceses to conform to national policy, like it or not. They didn't like it, and didn't conform. In 2007, San Joaquin voted to withdraw from the church and link up with a South American province of Anglicanism. Promptly the Episcopal Church's lawyers went to court, demanding the renegades leave their property behind. Again the Episcopal Church went to court when various Virginia parishes, disillusioned by the Gene Robinson affairs, voted to walk away. Go if you must, said the presiding bishop's office, but we're keeping the property. Other legal wars broke out on other fronts. Lawyers on both sides toiled far into the night, burnishing their briefs. Secular judges weighed and pondered. Christian vs. Christian: an odd testament, all in all, for public display to unbelievers.

No sympathy was noticeable for fellow Episcopalians who saw themselves unable—like the movie bank clerk ordered by robbers to open the vault—to embrace a form of ministry contrary to the design of God. Whatever He once might have led His people to believe, people today saw a new thing, which they embraced. Their proof was . . . that *they,* the Episcopal authorities, saw it. No one else had to. It was true for them, and so should it be for all Episcopalians.

Obsession with uniformity is no new thing in human affairs. We observe it all the time. Chiefly we discern it in the actions of those who have just routed from their trenches the defenders of an older order. The heat and intensity of the battle provide all the warrant necessary for coming down hard on the vanquished. Had they not fought so hard, resisted so long! But they did. So the French disciples of liberty, fraternity, and equality, with their eyes of steel and veins of marble, lopped off the heads of those less hot than themselves—and that covered lots of ground—for revolution and regicide. The scientific materialists of the Victorian age, their instinct carrying over to succeeding ages, looked askance at any who would claim a role for God in the perfection of human arrangements.

Of Christian theologians and pastors one might expect something more nearly resembling mercy than revenge and the chopping block. This is hardly the first expectation that today's Episcopal Church has dashed.

Postlude

THINK OF THE EPISCOPAL CHURCH AS A MIRROR: CHIC, SHIM-mering, artistically mounted. What do we do with mirrors? We hold them to our faces. We see ourselves, not always with undisguised pleasure, and some of the time with concern and dismay.

If the Episcopal Church mirrors to some large extent twenty-first-century American Christianity, what do twenty-first century American Christians learn by studying the reflection? Likely the consequences of too much absorption in the ideas and inspirations of the very fleeting moment. No single institution's experience parallels in precise detail another institution's. Yet under the broad canopy of culture, themes repeat themselves, notes, patterns, and rhythms.

From the 1950s through the start of the twenty-first century, liberation was American Christianity's theme. Christians were free to be free. If Episcopalians took more readily than many to the new environment of self-discovery and self-expression, it would have been odd had not others explored in the manner of their own choosing. As it happened, pretty much everyone took to exploring, even the Roman Catholics, with the Vatican II reforms that considerably loosened the reins held for centuries by clergy in directing spiritual affairs. The Catholic layman acquired scope not previously permitted him, such as the freedom to watch non-church approved movies and to decide what was for dinner on Fridays.

The civil rights crusade captivated other mainliners, though, as with the Episcopalians. Northerners were quicker than Southerners to embrace the cause. So, too, with the campaign to liberate women from deprivations and restrictions of various kinds.

I have not hitherto spoken of the divisions caused by the most divisive event in American history, the Vietnam War. That is because the war, a secular enterprise, with limited implications for religion, left only slight marks on Christian theology. War protest, broadly understood, was a matter more of visceral anger at "the power structure" than it was a consequence of Christian pacifist reasonings. Yet protest itself, broad and incessant, unsettled assumptions of authority, and of the deference owed or allotted the wielders of authority. In such an environment, authority of almost every sort, including the religious sort, was bound to come off badly.

For most churches, save those heavily emphasizing biblical authority, e.g., the Southern Baptists, women's issues were less stressful than inside the Episcopal fold, with its relatively high concept of priesthood. Observes Prof. Thomas Reeves, "Very few reasonable men wished to be seen as persecutors of women. . . . To be in favor of a male-only clergy caused one to be branded a sexist, a fundamentalist, a reactionary." So a woman wished to become a minister. Was that a matter worth dying for in the last ditch? Not as the American Baptist Convention and the United Presbyterians saw things. Both, in 1971, chose women as national leaders, as had the National Council of Churches two years earlier, in naming the Episcopalian Cynthia Wedel its president.

A significant consequence of mainline involvement with the cause of women's rights was mainline indifference toward calls to oppose the legalization of abortion. No other feminist claim equaled in vehemence the claim that a woman's right to "control" her body (as ratified, 7–2, by the U.S. Supreme Court) outranked an unborn child's right to enter the world alive. It was a claim that many religious supporters of feminism felt obliged to honor. To the defense of *Roe* v. *Wade* sprang the United Methodists, the United Presbyterians, the American Baptists, and the Congregationalists, as members of the Religious Coalition for Abortion Rights (now, more delicately, the Religious Coalition for Reproductive Rights). The Episcopal Church subsequently joined.

By contrast, which bodies have worked hardest for "pro-life" causes and objectives? Those with the slightest, most tenuous connections to ideological feminism—Roman Catholics and evangelicals, both of whom, while honoring women as men's spiritual equals, decline to view them living in a state of oppression, remediable only through total male surrender to their requests.

So also, when it comes to gay rights, these two unlikely groupings of Christians grasp hands in opposition to the new tenor of the times. Throughout much of modern society the moral equivalence of homosexuality and heterosexuality is a matter taken almost for granted, not only by Episcopalian leaders (and, of course, thorough-going secularists) but also by mainliners. Conservative resurgence within the United Methodist and United Presbyterian churches has had something to do with the mainline churches' failure to move as decisively as the Episcopalians did with the consecration of Bishop Gene Robinson. At the same time, no mainliner can say with utter confidence that the gay issue—the ultimate liberation issue, perhaps—will not one day rend the mainline churches like the veil of the temple. Such doubts, apprehensions, fears we may ascribe partly to the mirror effect: the reflection of Episcopal leaders stepping on or over fellow Episcopalians in their haste to create a new theological reality, namely, the moral equality of the gay and straight lifestyles.

What matter if, for example, the Presbyterians, in 1976, declared homosexuality sinful? Such a pronouncement, thirty years on, could be taken, and certainly has been, as mere evidence of mental paralysis in a fast-moving world. The way of liberation is the way of action. The way of action is the way of division. The way of division is the way of . . . might *destruction* qualify as one possibility?

Back to the Episcopal Church. We enter, closing the doors behind us. The scents and brassy splendor draw us farther inside. We sit. We kneel. We ponder how it could have come to this.

Granted, there are pitfalls in generalizing about two million alert and educated American Christians; still, what do we have? We have a church more visibly committed to cultural projects like "affirmation" and "inclusion" than to the task of conversion—conversion being, in fact, the enterprise diametrically opposite that of affirmation. That which you affirm—a mode of expression, a dubious belief—you decline to rebuke or convert. The affirming ways of the twenty-first-century Episcopal Church effectively sideline the church as an agent of spiritual renewal and transformation in a world, seemingly, in large need of transformation.

When, in 2006, the House of Bishops of the Episcopal Church elected Mrs. Jefforts Schori as presiding bishop, she wasted little time communicating her personal priorities for the church—priorities, it must be assumed, her supporters shared, or why would they have chosen her? In a newspaper interview she catalogued her passions, summarized by the reporter as "promoting peace and justice, eliminating poverty and hunger, making sure people have adequate sanitation, and treating people suffering with AIDS or other deadly diseases."

The name of Jesus went completely unmentioned in this accounting, as did any aspirations Mrs. Jefferts Schori might entertain concerning the spread of the Christian Gospel.

It would have seemed a very odd omission, indeed, to the robust Episcopal missionaries who took the sacraments and the prayer book to the mining camps and cattle towns of an earlier America, whose need for salvation through Jesus they took as somehow larger than anyone's expectation of three square meals a day. "I am the bread of life," Jesus had said. "He who comes to me will never hunger."

The oddness of Mrs. Jefferts Schori's catalogue consists in the unspoken implication that the Episcopal Church is the Peace Corps in ecclesiastical vestments. With maybe a new slogan: "Sanitation Now, Sanctification Later." The Jefferts Schori prescription satisfies secularist aspirations about the daily role of supernatural religion, through bypassing or downplaying the supernatural component that makes a church a church. It is as though the management of General Motors had decided to focus on the production of tarless cigarettes. It is more than that, in fact. Churches function on the basis of express directions from one who, as it happened, was the Son of God: "Do this in remembrance of me"; "Keep my commandments"; "Render therefore to Caesar the things that are Caesar's, and to God the things that are God's." A business may change its face with consequences only to itself, but not so a church, though the Episcopal Church of the twenty-first century might seem to be testing what it means to branch out, to "diversify" its domestic operations.

What, then? No non-ecclesiastical duties for the Episcopal Church, or, indeed, for any Christian church? That would be to drive the ox, and the argument, into the opposite ditch. The oddest feature, perhaps, of massive Episcopal disengagement from spiritual mission is the acute need for that which the church has uniquely to offer—the church, that is, as bearer of Christian truth, and with its deep understanding of the world to which it ministers, when it ministers rightly.

If the aftermath of the slaughter at the World Trade Center brought us nothing else useful, it invited attention to the character of religious commitment in the modern Christian West as contrasted with that in the Muslim East. As mosques rose in Europe's major cities, and as Europeans demonstrated a more profound attachment to soccer than to religion, warnings sounded. Was Christianity due for near-extinction on the continent most clearly identified for centuries with the religion of Christ?

For all their country's comparative religiosity, Americans, too, awoke to the phenomenon of resurgent secularism amid growing indifference to the core of the Christian message. By even the fragile standards of the 1950s, the Christianity of the twenty-first century could be called loose and lazy, with individuals going their own way, doing as they liked, and the mainstream churches uttering hardly a squeak of protest. If a state of crisis had indeed enveloped the culture, many Christians of the mainstream seemed hardly to notice. Sermons and budgets and action programs took more notice of social and economic challenges than of large hints that large numbers of Westerners simply didn't care what Christianity had to say about anything: sin, salvation, divorce, the Iraq War, homelessness, obesity, gasoline prices, subprime mortgages. Who needed the churches to tell them what Oprah had made clear already on her latest show?

To be American is, and ever has been, to leap from the armchair at the siren call of autonomy. To be a twenty-first-century American is to feel the daily surge of possibilities. Possibilities offered by the same God who poured brains and grit into His creations? That would be part of it, but only part, inasmuch as recognition of God's creative power involves recognition of His ultimate authority over creation.

Who's in charge here, anyway? That's the question, I think. On the Christian view the answer is God: "God the Father Almighty, Maker of heaven and earth." Yes, yes, but is the Big Fellow *really* in charge? And if so, what's in it for us? The deists of the seventeenth and eighteenth centuries, unduly impressed by the scientific achievements of the age, impressive as they certainly were, fashioned for their own satisfaction a God who in some unspecified measure had withdrawn from direct oversight of the world: possibly to put His feet on the desk and light up a Cuban cigar. This is neither the time nor the place to rehearse the history of Christianity from the eighteenth through the twentieth centuries. It suffices maybe to remark that in our time the connection between the Maker of heaven and earth, and those living on that part of the earth known as the West, is more tenuous than in quite a while.

Statistics show, in the United States if not yet in Europe, a strong and persistent commitment to God and Christ—strong in the formal sense of, yes, I read my Bible (sometimes), and, yes, I oppose the legalization of same-sex unions. As to how such a commitment shapes daily life in America, questions arise from time to time. Among them: Why, amid such religious commitment, so much acceptance of pornography, so much indifference, real or feigned, to illegitimacy and family brokenness? Why abortion as a constitutional right? Why the defiant secularism in so many quarters? Why the wranglings over Christian expression in public places like commencement exercises? Why religious ignorance as a way of life among millions of the young?

To ask such questions is in no way to ignore the large worshipping populations that appear in church every Sunday, or the growth curve of evangelical houses of worship, or the countless acts of service administered every day in Christ's name—healing for the sick, bread for the starving. I think that all the same no one can successfully deny that a forty-year-old culture of autonomy and liberation has had its way with our collective minds and hearts. The culture does not precisely wave a pistol in our faces, ordering us to bow down and worship. Still, it ensnares the thoughts that shape our actions.

But so what? If a culture such as ours—its motives and modes, its driving power—suits most of us well enough, where's the harm?

The collision of theory and reality, it seems to me, is the object for which we should be working and praying with extra diligence amid signs that theory is driving us straight toward disintegration.

That which *is*, as opposed to that which *seems,* enjoys no vogue in the twenty-first century, whose culture invites us to shape our own reality. Make that "realities." In this age of "truths," plural, as opposed to truth, singular, no duty binds us but that of tolerance. If I say "A" and another says "B," so be it, and bless us both. The religion of Christ instructs us differently. That is, it once did. The formal business of the religion of Christ is to give us an account of the reality that God has shaped for purposes utterly beyond us, and yet in some sense knowable, by means of—

I drag out, once more, Anglicanism's good old three-legged stool: Scripture, tradition, and reason. The most succinct account of all is in the Nicene Creed, to which I have alluded: a God, three in one and one in three, who created; who sent His only begotten Son to die for the sins of the world; who created, or had created in His name, a church to preserve and spread remembrance of these mighty works and promises, including the promise of a resurrection of the dead, unto everlasting life.

I think it might be agreed that not all human creatures receive the whole of this proposition, assuming they receive any at all. There is a larger point, nonetheless. It is that this account of reality—like it or not, differ with it or not, yell at it or not—is the Christian account. It is how, according to Christianity, things *are*. Never mind how they might be if we put our minds to it. Never mind how far behind, at voting time, the central account lags behind more populist alternatives. What God created is what God created, the only plausible response to that assertion being, what now?

Just here the church comes in. Or, that is, the divine intent, I believe. By "church," I mean any church, not just mine, the Episcopal variety. A church faithful to its calling will present to those who come within its ambit, on whatever business, *reality*. Not fantasy, certainly not that; not breezy speculation or wishful thinking, certainly not pandering or papering-over. For what would it profit a man were he to indulge every personal whim and lose his soul, a common and deadly consequence of over-indulgence? A church conscious of its obligation to the God it serves will, in its preaching and teaching, adhere strictly to the true and transcendent, however jagged the edges; this, for the sake of souls wholly dependent on the grace and mercy of God. It will reprove the deadly sins of pride, avarice, gluttony, wrath, and so on. It will applaud humility and obedience instead of power-seeking and self-fulfillment. It will describe to its listeners the stakes in this enterprise—life or death, separation from God or conformity to His purposes.

For performance of this grand undertaking, the church may should, expect scorn, coldness, hatred, and indifference, along with gratitude and thanksgiving. In accepting this very mixed bag, it will count itself blessed.

The specific case of the Episcopal Church is no easy one. Within Episcopalianism there is a seemingly unstoppable momentum to ratify the culture's choices—the whole range of them, centered on the plenary power of humans to ordain and dispense and control and rearrange. "Liberal" is not the right word to use, perhaps, in an ecclesiastical context, nor by the same token is "conservative," another term rising from our contests over worldly power. Yet, at Episcopal altars, and in Episcopal pews, the number of those who would generally describe themselves as liberal easily exceeds the number of those who want to "conserve." ("Conserve precisely what?" seems a logical question after four decades of church overhaul.)

Prospects for restoration of an Episcopal Church along the old lines—reverent, scholarly, open-minded within comprehensible limits—seem remote, though, of course, you never can be sure.

For now, I think there is profit in considering how a Christian church, bearing whatever name, might wish to confront and combat the degradations, paradoxes, and horrors of modern life. Life no worse in certain particular than at other times yet troubled in new and to some degree unprecedented ways.

The great trap that modern culture sets for humans is the description of human challenges as essentially human—that is, proceeding from particular conditions in the life of the present world. Thus the Katherine Jefferts Schori catalogue of challenges: hunger, sickness, sanitation, and so on, not to mention oppressions of various kinds, from which we have to liberate the victims, e.g., gays and lesbians. If we look at the religion of the Bible in this way, the viewpoints of people who wore strange costumes, ate strange foods, and spoke a strange language seem—whatever the word for it, the feeling is of distance and space rather than intimacy and nearness. Have the apostles anything useful to teach the people of the Blackberry-and-Botox era?

Well, yes. That would be the answer, all right—a hard answer, nevertheless, to make apparent when the alternatives are, seemingly, stained-glass stagnation on the one hand, dynamic social and cultural engagement on the other hand. My own pained observation is that too few proclaimers of the Christian gospel, whether "liberal" or "conservative," ever establish a decisive connection between the religion they preach and the lives of those to whom they preach it.

To look at the matter another way, is there a contingency in all-human occasions? Does that contingency, if it exists, arise from human dependence on the purposes of the Creator God? For instance, take the relationship between the sexes. Is the main question, *who runs the show around here*? Or is the question more slippery: *What is the show about*? Has God a stake in the outcome? The Christian churches of the United States grow tongue-tied at the notion of actually rebuking sins that lack a political foundation. For Episcopalians, as for large numbers of other Christians, the paramount issues are sex and sexual expression, neither viewed by the culture as means to a larger end but as *the* end—the rapturous, ravishing meaning of life.

Small problem here. Suppose, on the supernatural view of things, that God created man and woman, whether Edenically or in primordial ooze, for purposes that might properly be described as His own, involving the raising up of generation after generation consecrated to those purposes. Here would be something entirely different from Better Sex, Protected Sex, Recreational

Sex, Sex as Power, Sex as—I think, here, of our wrestlings with homosexual rights—Personal Identity. Might we not suppose the church had some obligation to sort through these questions and pronounce in order to guide? And yet, in the Episcopal context, on such occasions as there is talk of sex, the talk is of "rights" and putative threats to those "rights."

The church of God seems to characterize the question of God's design for human life as arising not least under the life, liberty, and property clause of the Fourteenth Amendment to the U.S. Constitution. Not a few of our priests, it strikes me, may have missed their true vocation as lawyers or congressmen.

To the guardianship of human life, the Episcopal Church hardly pretends. Witness the protective cloak it throws over abortion-seekers. The religious language that it brings to the discussion ("Through our mutual desires for one another we can, by God's grace, be drawn into the love which is of God") has the appearance of window-dressing, put out in order to meet the expectation that a church will bring a little of the sort to any major discussion. Where, by contrast, is the deep analysis, seasoned with the reflections of Christian theologians from the first century A.D. to the present day?

Where, likewise, is the reasoned analysis of the materialist temptation ("Buy this in remembrance of me," as it was parodied by Malcolm Muggeridge)? A nearly as common temptation is that of denouncing "economic inequality" from the pulpit without accompanying reflection on the differences between moral and economic inequality (cf. *Luke* 21:1-4) or on the responsibilities of stewardship (unless, to be sure, it's Stewardship Month). And yet the vices of materialism and consumerism would seem almost uniquely logical topics for thoughtful—as opposed to ideological—guidance in this most prosperous of eras. How do we respectfully use that which God has given us?

Brooding, it may be, above all other topics is terrorism of the sort that seems to arise from religious motives. This is not least because the habit of many modern Christians is to shrink from asserting that anyone's religion—especially, perhaps, their own—deserves priority over anyone else's. As Mrs. Jefferts Schori has put it, "We who practice the Christian tradition understand [Jesus] as our vehicle to the divine. But for us to assume that God could not act in other ways is, I think, to put God in an awfully small box." So much for evangelism and conversion! Yet the moral equivalence of all religions is not a point much in favor with Islamic terrorists. Nor should Christians fail to notice in secular, desacralized Europe how successful are the Muslims, with their hard, fierce faith, at engineering the voluntary conversion of post-Christians for whom, thitherto, religion had barely existed.

Islam's comparative successes in the heart of Western culture vex no explanation. What could seem finer to the imams than Christianity's voluntary withdrawal to the cultural sidelines, its growing disinclination to talk about the Christian distinctives— a virgin birth, a resurrection, grace, forgiveness, redemption. In modern times, daily life has come to resemble an alternative reality: way over there, over the horizon, the kingdom of God, with its tinkling harps, but over here, a world interested in the world itself, checking itself constantly in the mirror for signs of anxiety or sagging flesh.

To large numbers, the notion of living with heaven always in view is strictly an acquired taste, with nothing to do with terrorism, or interest rates, or the Social Security crisis, or control of Congress, or early admission to a good college.

So the world trudges on, often enough with the encouragement of the Christian churches, to confront its specific predicaments by its own specific lights. The relevance of heaven, and of the Bible, and of the Sacraments, to the confronting of those predicaments is a possibility I doubt anyone would claim to be overemphasized in Christian pulpits or Christian publications.

What might the churches, if they were serious about the sacred enterprise to which they are called, actually bring to the addressing of the human predicament? A variety of things, given the variousness, not to mention the durability, of human predicaments. (Nor have I anything in mind as witless as theocracy—control of human affairs by the same people, many of them, whose views on affairs I have had occasion already to question).

I have in mind two things, essentially:

1. A sense of proportion, of God as indeed the God of the Creeds, to whom all is owed, from whom come all things. Once upon a time Episcopalians (in the context of Morning Prayer, when it was a more central service than now) sang on Sundays, "We praise thee O God, we acknowledge thee to be the Lord. All the earth doth worship thee, the Father everlasting. To thee all angels cry aloud, the heavens and all the powers therein." It was possible to turn one's back on such a God. Possible, but potentially ruinous. Jesus as "vehicle to the divine" might be an eschewable habit—not so Jesus as redeemer and judge. The victory, in men's minds, of the one over the other seems unlikely to produce a faith tough and tensile enough to stand a culture on its head. "Oh, please, approve of me"—the usual message of modern Christian churches—makes a feeble substitute for "I am the way, and the truth, and the life; no one comes to the Father, but by me." The trouble with Christianity is not flamboyance of conviction. The trouble is paucity of conviction, flaccidity, the turned cheek replaced by a "Kick Me" sign. It is, at the lowest level, failure to believe all—or to believe at all.

2. A sense of humility. As it happens, this sense flows straight from the aforementioned sense of God as ruler of all. The hierar-

chical view of anything sits poorly with a hyper-democratic culture. Humility suggests inequality. I would reply: So? We seek equality with God? If memory serves, so did Satan. We see how well that gambit worked out, and what its consequences proved to be. The Book of Common Prayer—and especially the older versions thereof—is full of language that daily reinforces the old narrative of man's just dependence on the grace and mercy of his Father in Heaven.

"And there is no health in us," the old General Confession justly acknowledged. Naturally, that wouldn't do for the Age of Self-Esteem. Away went this piece of self-abasement. Yet the genuine and essential piety of the old book—the sense of unfitness it preached, of unworthiness, if you like, or even don't like—survives in large degree and might yet serve to ground a revival of the luminousness and gratitude that came with the confession of human powerlessness. In the words of the Collect for the Third Sunday in Lent: "Almighty God, who seest that we have no power of ourselves to help ourselves." And in other collects, over and over again: "[G]ive us grace to cast away the works of darkness"; "that we, being regenerate and made thy children by adoption and grace"; "giving us those good things which we are not worthy to ask"; "Make speed to help thy servants"; "Lighten our darkness"; "Give unto thy servants that peace which the world cannot give."

It is all there still, as tense and strong and vital and God-given as ever. What might all our churches of the Christian mainline—what might my Episcopal Church—do at this moment for their own sakes, for the sake of the many who look to them for the words of salvation? They might start once more to believe with all their heart, the way they once did believe. Believe what? The words their followers and servants took centuries ago to forests and fields and cabins, for their own part believing such words, such promises, to bear the stamp of God, to be the very words of life spoken to His faithful people.

Then, and—oh, yes, certainly, positively, beyond the remotest question—now.

Index